PROMISES
TO KEEP

PROMISES TO KEEP

A Call for a
New American Revolution

Richard N. Goodwin

G

3908204996061/3

ISBN: 8129-2054-6
LC: 92-53674

Manufactured in the United States of America
9 8 7 6 5 4 3 2
First Edition

To Arnold Hiatt—
good friend and exemplar
of the principled life

I muse upon my country's ills—
The tempest bursting from the waste of Time.

Nature's dark side is heeded now
A child may read the moody brow
Of yon black mountain lone.
With shouts the torrents down the gorges go,
And storms are formed behind the storm we feel:
The hemlock shakes in the rafter,
   the oak in the driving keel.

—HERMAN MELVILLE,
from "Misgivings" (1860)

Contents

PROMISES
TO KEEP

I

Broken Promises

AMERICA WAS CONCEIVED not merely as a land to be inhabited and exploited, but as an idea and a great experiment, as a home where men and women could be free, joined in one nation by a common dream. From our earliest days we have been a great nation—not because of our mounting material wealth and military power, but because of our dedication to Thomas Jefferson's assertion that "the equal rights of man and the happiness of every individual, are now acknowledged to be the only legitimate objects of government." It was this conviction that brought thousands and then millions to these shores—trusting that if they gave of their toil, courage, skill, and faith they could build a more spacious and abundant life for future generations.

The years following the Second World War seemed to confirm this belief. In two and a half decades, median family income nearly doubled, and a growing economy sustained America's strength and its greatness among the nations. Expressing a conviction shared by the large majority of Americans during the 1950s, Vice President Richard M. Nixon asserted "that the United States, the world's largest capitalist country, from the standpoint of the distribution of wealth comes closest to the ideal of prosperity for all in a classless society."

The buoyant hopes of postwar America, a modern expression of the founders' dream, now have been replaced by decline and uncertainty, and by apprehension bordering on fear. And the fear is justified. Something has gone seriously wrong. Since our earliest years, the promise, the meaning of America has included opportunity for every citizen. And American opportunity has always meant more than a chance to receive the bare necessities of life. It meant no citizen was shackled to a fixed position in the structure of society. It was a chance to grow, to enrich the quality of life, to ensure even larger possibilities for one's children. But that expectation— the American promise—is being betrayed.

For almost a quarter-century the standard of American life has been diminishing. The growth in well-being that we regarded as our destiny and our birthright as Americans has halted and gone into decline. Increasing numbers of our fellow citizens must struggle to maintain what they have already achieved, and for many it is a losing battle. The past twenty years have been a time of decline for the great majority of our people. And now economic growth has come to a halt, while opportunity has been severely eroded. America's descent already afflicts all those who are not protected from deterioration by the control of wealth or public power.

The promise that is America is being taken away.

Should our decline continue, then the freedom for which this nation was created will be diminished. For the meaning of freedom is given content by concepts like "opportunity" and "justice." Long before Marx, Voltaire said that the commerce that had enriched the citizens of England had helped to make them free, and that freedom in turn had encouraged commerce; this had produced the greatness of the British state. In our own time, the Soviet Union and its former satellites have been transformed by the realization that the opportunity to lead a more fulfilling life is inseparable from political freedom. Their struggle has been fueled by the great and incontestable lesson of the American experience. We must not now neglect in our own land that which we have taught to a continent of oppression. Thus the stakes in a battle to change America are very high: not merely prosperity and opportunity, justice and a decent existence for all our people, but that sovereign principle which they help sustain—the greatness which is the gift of freedom.

America is today amid what economists and political leaders choose to call a recession. The word implies a temporary dip in the economic cycle from which we will reascend to recovery as a prelude to growth and mounting prosperity. But there is no justification for such optimistic beliefs. The term "recession" itself is a relic of an America that has receded into history. Our present distress is not the transitory interruption of an ascending destiny, but the visible, increasingly dramatic manifestation of a deterioration that began about two decades ago, a consequence of fundamental defects and spreading corruption in our political and economic system.

We may well have a temporary "recovery," but it will not last. For the foundation that has sustained the well-being of the nation and its people has been eroded by greed, corruption, complacency, and simple failure to adapt to the exigencies of a changing world economy.

Since the founding of the Republic, an improving standard of living, a fuller and more abundant existence, has been the goal of America. And we have moved steadily toward that goal. Until now. Until the present decline, which will—despite all the prophecies of "experts"—continue unless we mobilize to arrest and reverse it.

Over the last two decades the income of most Americans has stagnated or declined. Yet the money we earn is the most important component of our American "standard of living," or of our "quality of life." It is our exchange—for a home, a warm room with a rug on the floor, a dishwasher that works, the time to raise our children and to indulge some of the wants of childhood, to send our kids to college or vocational schools, and to enjoy the manifold pleasures of leisure time. If we are not able to make a decent living, our lives and sense of worth are drained of much of their meaning. Our "pursuit of happiness" is reduced to a struggle to maintain the barest amenities of life, and we are continually consumed by fear that rent or mortgage payments will be overdue, that family food budgets are too small for sound nutrition, that our children will be deprived of the chance to learn or to find a rewarding job. These conditions are not the stuff of American freedom.

Yet, even though our current distress is usually described in economic terms, the "standard of American life" cannot be measured solely by personal income or increased wealth. Over the last quarter-century, for most of us, it has also been diminished by devastation of our connection to the natural world and by the waste of our children's possibilities in poor school systems. It has been injured by the violence that has made us feel less secure in our homes and on the streets, while the emergence of inner-city "ghettos"—home to poverty, violence, and drugs—is an assault on the American values which sustain our pride. Nor can individuals, acting alone, restore those weakening bonds that have linked us to family, neighborhood, and community. All these and more have already been impaired by the deterioration of American society. Since these deteriorations in our "standard of living" are, in part, both cause and consequence of our decline, they too are "economic."

Recently I made a visit to Revere Beach on Boston's North Shore, where as a child I had learned to swim while my cautious and proud parents looked on. I approached the water and noticed that, despite the midsummer heat, there was no one swimming. A scattering of garbage—discarded cans, wrappers, a blood-soaked tampon—deterred me from taking off my shoes. At the sea's edge, where the familiar surf broke gently over some nearby sandbars, I saw that what a child had viewed as an inviting iridescence had turned an ominous brown, scattered with oily patches. An old man hobbled by. He waved, and called out: "Don't go in there, you'll get AIDS!"

"You don't get AIDS from water," I said.

"Then you'll get something else. It all comes from the sewer pipes," he replied, and pointed to a line of condominiums along the beachfront. "Nobody goes in, except some crazy kids late at night. Not much for swimming. Not bad for walking, though—it's cooler close to the water. Just don't get too close."

He walked on, humming cheerfully as if God were in his heaven and all was right with the world. But my Revere Beach—once the principal resort for young people jamming the subways from city neighborhoods on hot summer days for a day of fun at the shore—was gone. And for those who lived there, and those who might once have come there from Boston, the quality of life had been diminished. Their standard of living had declined. And the richest man in the entire county could not have afforded to extract a significant portion of that brownish poison from the ocean waters.

I do not believe that this corrosion in the sustaining structure of our democracy has progressed beyond our capacity for restoration. We remain a strong and resourceful people. We are the descendants of those who successfully confronted equally serious assaults on the principles of the na-

tion and the well-being of its citizens. But like the struggle
to preserve the Union little over a century ago, or to overcome the Depression of the 1930s, the task will require
drastic changes carried out by a people united in determination, and a willingness to accept present sacrifice for the
future's sake.

For the sources of today's assault on the seminal principles
of opportunity and justice cannot be overcome by simple
modifications of existing public policies. Transferring money
from arms to education, enlarging benefits to the unemployed, or extending health care may be desirable, and would
enhance the lives of many individuals. But such changes in
policy—which now dominate what passes for public dialogue—will not arrest a process of decay that results from
deepening flaws in the structure that sustains our society: It is
like debating what color to paint the house, or how to
remodel the porch, when the foundation is crumbling.

Our future depends on the ability to mount a struggle for
extensive, even drastic changes in the institutions that compose both the private economy and the process of politics
and government, along with the intricate web of relationships that connect them with each other and with the people. Changes so fundamental are revolutionary. But such
revolutions pervade the entire chronicle of America. They
have fueled our growth and progress while enabling us to
sustain fidelity to the principles of American freedom. In
time, even the most productive systems are outstripped by
changes in the nation and in the world, and that is what has
happened to today's America.

When the system is malfunctioning and the well-being of
the citizen, the health of the society, and the greatness of
the nation are in danger, we must be willing to demand
far-reaching changes in the structure itself. Such an effort
will provoke opposition and calumny from those who have

aggrandized themselves through their control of the existing sources of power. It always has. A movement for drastic and fundamental change will inevitably be condemned as "radical." And so it is. But such radicalism is woven into the fabric of our history; it is a recurrent motif in the two-century chronicle of freedom. It is an essential part of the American tradition. If we are to be faithful to that tradition, we must act, as our ancestors did, to alter the structure of society so we may conserve those formative principles that have guided the American voyage.

This mandate was implicit in Jefferson's conviction that "each generation is as independent of the one preceding as that was of all which had gone before. It has, then, like them, a right to choose for itself the form of government it believes most promotive of its own happiness; consequently to accommodate to the circumstances in which it finds itself, that it received from its predecessors." Even amid his greatest triumphs, Jefferson foresaw that new conditions and alterations of popular desire would require modification, even revolutionary changes, in the structure his generation had so brilliantly conceived and laboriously erected.

Jefferson's expression of principle was also a prophecy. During every significant period in American history, the dominant economic structures have been drastically altered from those that came before. American history shows a constant process of change in the structure that defines relationships between government and the economy, between government and the people. Some of the changes were a natural evolution; others the result of popular demand and political leadership.

In the 1930s, for example, the New Deal irretrievably reshaped the relationship between government and private enterprise. Banking was subjected to new limits and rules of conduct. ("I have to save the bankers from committing suicide," Roosevelt remarked.) A new regulatory system was imposed on the securities industry, and a new agency (the Securities and Exchange Commission) established for enforcement. Social Security protected workers from the threat of impoverishment because of advancing age. Government programs put millions of the unemployed to work on constructive projects. (I once lived in a small Connecticut town where the only ice-skating rink, a continuing source of recreation and pleasure, had been built by the Works Progress Administration.) The National Youth Administration gave impoverished youngsters a chance to acquire skills and perform useful work and, not incidentally, helped to shape the abilities and philosophy of a future President of the United States.

"When I ran the NYA down in my part of Texas," Lyndon Johnson once said, "it was not only good for the kids, it was good for me. I saw government could help people. I worked day and night, and they appreciated it, and I think I did some good. There weren't very many, and they needed me. But I was torn. I couldn't look into those hopeful faces without wanting to rush straight to Washington to help Roosevelt help everyone. He was always my hero." Some thirty years later, when President Johnson addressed Congress and the nation to demand that all black Americans be guaranteed the right to vote, he chose to conclude his argument by invoking his youthful experience with the NYA as evidence that, given hope, the despised and abandoned could be transformed into ambitious and productive citizens.

All this, and more, was accomplished despite vehement resistance and dire prophecies from our most powerful economic institutions. "No other word than hatred will do," wrote journalist Marquis Childs in 1936, referring to Franklin Roosevelt. "Here is no mere political opposition, no mere disagreement over financial policies . . . It is a consuming personal hatred . . . which permeates . . . the whole upper stratum of American society." Yet the year before Childs wrote, corporate profits had increased 40 percent. And the ultimate result of the New Deal was to restore and strengthen American capitalism, enlarge the possibilities of the American future, and provide a foundation for the enormous economic achievements of the Second World War. Revolutionary change had, in fact, preserved both capitalism and democracy. The American system of democratic capitalism would be maintained and, ultimately, would begin once again to thrive.

Democracy and capitalism are the twin pillars of American society. Together they support the structure that guards and advances the traditional purposes of American life: national growth in the service of democratic values; increasing opportunity for every individual to sustain and enhance his life; economic justice for every citizen; and the protective strengthening of those ties that have traditionally bound us to our fellow citizens and to the heritage and destiny of the nation.

Democracy, the first of our supporting pillars, grants every American the right to choose the managers of government, to hold them to account for their stewardship, and to ensure they serve the interests of the entire citizenry. Democracy is the political system by which the governed consent to their government, through which the collective will of the people can be expressed, and which protects the general welfare against the abuses of private power. It is government of, by, and for the people.

Capitalism, our second pillar, is the engine for the creation and distribution of wealth. It is based on the right to private property acquired and used within an open and competitive marketplace. Properly subject to democratic restraints, it has rewarded those who add to the wealth and well-being of the nation, whether they found a great enterprise, work on the assembly line, or till the land. It has stimulated the development of new business and industry. And it was, as it still remains, the source of the citizens' opportunity to sustain and enhance their lives.

The founding principles of democracy and capitalism are indissolubly linked; both are essential to the freedom and well-being of American society. But they are not equals. There are many sources of power in America, but the people alone are sovereign. Those chosen to lead the institutions of democracy are only the trustees of that sovereignty.

Democracy alone can ensure freedom of the marketplace, justice in the distribution of wealth, equality of opportunity to contribute and receive a fair reward for skill and labor. It is responsible for protecting the people against abuses of private economic power, for preserving an open and competitive market, and for ensuring that capitalism serves the interests of the entire American community. "Nature is the great democrat," Justice Felix Frankfurter said, meaning that intelligence and vitality were bestowed on the children of rich and poor alike, "but it is only the structure of American society that lets these qualities find fulfillment."

Yet this authority of government does not conflict with the reality that capitalism, as we have known it, is a necessary condition of political democracy. Free enterprise and free markets—as is widely known and understood—prevent the ingathering of wealth and control over wealth into a few hands, a concentration that would inevitably convey with it the power to manipulate and pervert the process of democratic rule. It is no coincidence, but necessity, that the explosion of democracy in Eastern Europe and elsewhere has been accompanied by the demand for "free enterprise" and "free markets," for one cannot exist without the other. Those who helped create the American nation understood that the separation of public and private power was essential, not only to democratic freedom but to a thriving economy whose growth would enlarge opportunity for all citizens. All private interests had the right to be represented in government, but none to usurp the authority bestowed on the institution of democratic rule.

Yet in recent decades we have transgressed this seminal principle. To a significant extent, private power has subordinated the structures of representative democracy to the service of its own interests. It has bridged the division that has been essential to shared prosperity. The result—wholly predictable—has been that a few have flourished while the nation as a whole, the common well-being, has begun to deteriorate. Our welfare, and perhaps that of our children, has been damaged by a profane combination of private interests with public authority that has corrupted the system upon which opportunity and the quality of life depend. That combination violates the spirit and tradition of America. It betrays the intention of the Constitution, the purpose of those who framed it, and the sometimes painful and dangerous struggles of those generations whose fidelity to these animating convictions made it possible for a struggling young nation to defeat the enemies obstructing its rise to greatness.

The promise of America was fulfilled over generations not simply because fortune had granted us a large and abundant land. Other nations, similarly gifted, failed to provide their people with the possibilities of an enhanced existence. Our achievements were made possible by democratic freedom, which required the subordination of all private power to the sovereignty of popular rule. It is a tragic irony that as others now struggle to emulate us, we have begun to abandon the system that vivified our own advance.

Although belief in the right to private property was among their firmest convictions, the worldly and intelligent architects of America rejected the "invisible hand" of Adam Smith, which postulated that the pursuit of individual self-interest must inevitably serve the general interest. Instead, the general interest was to be guaranteed by the sovereign power of the people. The rights of property—essential both to freedom and to economic growth—were to be made to serve the prosperity of the entire American community by the restraining powers of representative democracy. This required, the Framers warned, that the boundary between economic and political power—being vulnerable—must be sedulously maintained and vigilantly guarded; that its breach could well lead to the ascendancy of "faction," or special economic interests, which, as Madison explained, "are united . . . by . . . interests adverse to the right of other citizens, or to the permanent and aggregate interests of the community." Even the most ingeniously crafted democratic structures could not, by themselves, guarantee a free people irrevocable exemption from the depredations of "faction." "Men of factious temper, of local prejudices, or of sinister designs," Madison cautioned, "may, by intrigue, by corruption, or by other means, first obtain the suffrages, and then betray the interests of the people." Jefferson likewise exhorted his colleagues that "we must put it out of the power of the few to riot on the labors of the many."

The most reliable guardian of democracy was not the careful limitation and division of powers, the "checks and balances" between deliberately varied political institutions. The Framers knew that no design for democratic government could be proof against dangers from a future whose circumstances could not be foreseen. Thus, they bestowed the supreme power to protect democracy on the people, whose sovereignty—ultimate and irreversible—would ordinarily, but not exclusively, be guaranteed and exercised through "the restraint of frequent election."

However, even the most gifted among the Framers could not have foreseen the extravagance of today's contests for public office, or that the interests of the people might be betrayed not only by intrigue or corruption, but by the anxiety to retain the powers and privileges of office, and the incapacity of officials to understand the interests of the people. Yet all of these have come to pass. Corruption, anxiety for office, and mediocrity rule the land. They preside over the current decline in the promise of American life.

The dissolution of political restraints has led, as the founders feared, to the increasing ascendancy of "faction," enabling a few to manipulate the governing structure of wealth and politics so as to aggrandize themselves at the expense of the many. The result has been to weaken the basic principles and process of American democratic capitalism, which were designed to reward the most efficient and productive, to ensure a freely competitive market, to allow access to new enterprise, and to provide employment and opportunity for all.

Since the structure of democratic capitalism—the system itself—has now been ruptured, healing and restoration will require large and drastic changes. They will not come easily. They require a struggle to overcome, first ourselves—the doubt or disbelief that we have the power to change the country—and then the formidable opposition of those factions that have feasted on the very sources of our decline and enriched themselves at the expense of the people and the grandeur of the nation.

Because our problems are so profoundly rooted in the

present structure, we cannot hope to reduce distress—much less achieve enduring change—by electing still another set of candidates supported by the same special interests as those officials they hope to succeed, their loyalty pledged to parties that differ only over minor modifications to a failing system and in the deceptive stridency of their calculated and empty rhetoric. The great political debates over national destiny—Hayne versus Webster; the League of Nations; the New Deal versus unrestrained enterprise—have faded into history. Both major parties have supported the failed policies of recent decades. Neither offers a persuasive choice of measures that might avert further descent. We no longer have a two-party system.

There are, of course, two major political organizations with different names. But, with several honorable exceptions, members of both parties gratefully receive huge campaign contributions from the same sources; rely for election on the wealth and power of the same factions; serve the same interests. Nor are campaign contributions the only source of corruption by money. There is an ingeniously contrived multitude of profitable "special arrangements" between business and politicians—sweetheart contracts; "loans" made without expectation of repayment; land deals; free "use" or "loan" of business services, facilities, and equipment. Indeed, it seems that almost every day's paper discloses some new example of a political official reaping financial gain from private interests.

The bifurcation of Republicans and Democrats is necessary to provide an institutional structure for election contests and political advancement. Our existing parties are a necessary conduit for personal ambition and provide the competitive struggles essential to enhance the power of those private interests that finance campaigns. But election contests between candidates whose only real difference is their party label are a travesty. Without substantial divisions of ideology, there is no choice to be made. And without choice there is no democracy; only a system that entertains us with the trappings of a contest between different men for the same power.

Those who have acted to diminish the nation—businessmen, bankers, politicians, and others who possess public power—have forfeited their claim to leadership. The organs of representative democracy themselves seem increasingly impotent to fulfill their constitutional obligations. They have been paralyzed, in part corrupted, by powerful interests that aggrandize themselves at the expense of the public good. The very political structures designed to prevent the abuse of the many by those factions that control concentrated wealth and private power have become their servants and accomplices in the deterioration of American life. They have demonstrated their incapacity to govern in accordance with the principles that brought us greatness.

We cannot hope to restore America by electing the "right" person to the White House, or by awaiting the emergence of an inspiring liberator.

"What if I did get to be President," Robert Kennedy once remarked at the end of a long day of primary campaigning in Indiana, "how could I ever get done what I want with Congress, the press, business always pressing down on you?" The doubt was honest and justified. But it was quickly put aside. It was late, and, in a few hours, another campaign day would begin. No one could endure the rigors of campaigning unless he believed the power he sought was real. And so the candidate forced himself to believe it. But if Robert Kennedy perceived such obstacles in 1968, how much larger are the obstructions in today's America?

We must not indulge ourselves in the belief that somehow, in some magically unforeseeable way, life-enhancing progress will return. Resigning his commission after defeating the British at Yorktown, Washington wrote that "the Citizens of America . . . are . . . to be considered the Actors on a most conspicuous Theatre, which seems to be peculiarly designed by Providence for the display of human greatness and felicity . . . if [our] citizens should not be completely free and happy the fault will be entirely their own." Washington's admonition must become our guide. Today's distress is our fault. And we alone can remedy it.

To that end, I propose the formation of a new movement for democratic capitalism to help mobilize all those who are aware of mounting unfairness, economic injustice, dangerous class divisions, and an ominous descent in the possibilities and principles of American life. Its purpose is to strike off the shackles that now confine the energies and skills of a great people, liberating them to restore the America to which they were born and to which their forefathers sailed. Only a movement of the people, joined in common determination and organized toward a common purpose, can hope to overthrow the combination of concentrated privilege and the political process that continues to assault the greatness of the nation and the fair expectations of its people.

Mounting such a popular revolution is not a radical departure from the American experience. The Declaration of Independence, which created this nation, asserts that when any form of government diminishes our rights to life, liberty, or the pursuit of happiness, "it is the Right of the People to alter . . . it." The Constitution and the principles of our democratic government bestow the ultimate sovereignty on the people alone. When our governing structure fails to meet the needs of the American people, diminishes the greatness of the nation, contributes to widening and destructive divisions between races, classes, and interests, then

18

it is the unalienable right of the people to strip the governors of their power, and require that the nation be restored to its citizens. Our history discloses a multitude of such enterprises. The Minutemen, the Populists, the civil-rights movement, the peace movement, the women's movement are only a few examples among many of the power of an aroused people to overcome injustice or oppression rooted in powerfully established institutions.

The immediate intention of this new movement is not necessarily to elect candidates to office (although it may ultimately undertake such efforts), but to compel political leaders to change course and to serve the interests of the people they were elected to serve. The objectives and the unifying purposes of such a movement are discussed in some detail throughout the pages of this essay. Specific proposals for change are offered as suggestions toward formulating a practical agenda. Further discussion will doubtless improve and supplement what is set forth here as a way of initiating action and debate.

Only one thing is not debatable: the urgency of the need for action. The American community is being sundered, each further separation breeding hostility. Our resources and the quality of individual life continue to diminish. The time to act is now upon us, before divisions are so instilled with enmity that they cannot be healed, before decay progresses even beyond our abundant capacity to restore America.

We must not wait for acknowledged leaders—persons who are widely recognized and respected—to step forward and take command. Our entire history instructs us that when abuse of principle requires a movement for change, that movement begins with the people. This country has often been changed from the bottom up, by causes that have given voice and hope to beliefs already held. Joined in such a cause, a people moved to action by shared grievances and determination will not long lack for leaders. Out of protest and anger, out of the gathered demands of an aroused people, out of action and marches and an abundance of voices summoning the justly aggrieved, leaders will emerge, created by the people they lead. Even now those who will guide the American restoration undoubtedly await, unaware that the moment of opportunity is approaching, not suspecting that history has marked a place for them.

On a bright spring day in 1775 an anonymous young American farmer grasped his musket as he confronted the red-coated British regulars across the small wooden bridge that spans the tranquil Concord River. No one, on either side, was eager for a battle; yet that young man, suddenly shaken, perhaps by some unexpected noise from the riverbank—a twig snapped by a darting squirrel, a brook trout breaking the surface—felt an almost uncontrollable spasm constrict his finger, heard the gases explode from his musket, then the fusillade that followed. And all North America had been changed.

A little less than two centuries later, a black woman took a seat toward the front of a bus in Montgomery, Alabama. As other passengers entered, the driver turned toward her and gestured. She knew what the gesture meant. She was to give up her place and take a seat at the back of the bus, where Negroes were consigned. I can only guess what went through her mind. For years, she must have seen that gesture and obediently, almost mechanically, moved to the back. But not today. Something stirred. She felt an impulse as swiftly unexpected as that which had seized the young American farmer long before she was born, the descendant of slaves. And what stirred that impulse—resentment, some idea of freedom, or just some subtle provocation in the expression of the bus driver that made it unexpectedly imperative to assert her humanity? *You may kill me or jail me, but you will have to punish me. Not a "rebel" or a "Negro" but me, Rosa Parks of Montgomery.*

"I'm a dreamer," Lyndon Johnson once told a meeting of his immediate staff, "You boys are dreamers too. Every American has a little bit of dream in him. But it's not like those Harvards think. It's not enough to sit around and dream, and criticize things you don't like. You've got to do something about it, in the real world. That's why we're here." Johnson was right to observe that every American shared in the dream. It remains true, even today, when that dream is under unremitting assault. But it is equally true that realization requires practical action; more now than when the President spoke, since the problems are so much larger, more deeply rooted. We do not need more heartfelt words or more lies, good intentions or broken promises. The answer today, as it has been in the past, is to reexamine and revise the structure of democratic capitalism in America.

II

The Triumph of Money and the Ascendancy of Faction

MANY YEARS AGO I flew over the extravagantly fertile central valley of Chile. A large proportion of the most productive land lay fallow, abandoned by absentee landlords, many of whom made their homes in the most favored neighborhoods of Paris or London. Tiny plots of this land were reserved for tenant farmers—sharecroppers—who were compelled to exchange their labor for the right to till the property. Lacking any effective system of marketing and distribution, the sharecroppers brought their crops to market and sold them at an insignificant fraction of their real value. The farmer's entire life was a laborious struggle for subsistence. Yet Chile was a "capitalist" country: private property, open markets. But the fruits of capitalist production were restricted to a favored few. Although the Chile I saw was a capitalist country, it was one so different from the United States as to demonstrate that capitalism is not a universally fixed form of economy; it is mutable. Rooted in the private ownership of property and some form of market competition, it derives its qualities from the culture it dominates.

In America, as in Chile, the creation of wealth is the business of business. But the principles and traditions of

American democracy tell us that wealth is not an end in itself. It is the means through which citizens have the opportunity to enhance their lives and build for the future—their own and that of generations to follow. It is the source of what we know as the American standard of living.

American capitalism has been firmly, indissolubly wed to democracy. Property, and the right to acquire it, belongs to individuals. But the process through which wealth is created and distributed—what is permitted and how—is ultimately subject to the control of the people, acting through democratic institutions. When it is functioning well, each aspect of this single process—democracy and capitalism—reinforces and strengthens the other. Government is democracy's instrument to prevent capitalism from becoming the private preserve of a few and to open its wealth-creating possibilities to all our people.

In that sense, in America, capitalism is democracy. Assets, wealth, businesses are not in private hands simply because economies work better that way. More important is that the separation of economic from political power is necessary to freedom, just as their fusion is the progenitor of despotism. Both property and democracy are derived from the resources and people of a single land. And in a free country, where the people alone are sovereign, all power must be subject to the ultimate control of democracy, its laws and institutions.

As Lord Cornwallis strode forward to surrender his army at Yorktown, bringing the American war for independence to a successful conclusion, the British band ironically marked the astonishing ceremony by playing "The World's Turned Upside Down." The world of today's American society has also turned upside down. Large private interests, constitutional subjects of democratic control, have become its masters—not wholly, but enough to prevent government from meeting the most urgent needs and advancing the welfare of the American community.

The principal power in Washington is no longer the government or the people it represents. It is the money power. Under the elaborately deceptive cloak of campaign contributions, access and influence, votes and amendments are bought and sold. Money establishes priorities of action, holds down federal revenues, revises economic legislation, shifts income from the middle class to the very rich. Money restrains the enforcement of laws written to protect the country from the abuses of wealth—laws that mandate environmental protections; antitrust laws; laws to protect the consumer against fraud; laws that safeguard the securities market; and many more.

As the cost of campaigning rises—and it is continually increasing—so does the need for money. The more money is needed, the larger the expected return, the more numerous those to whom something is "owed," and the more powerful are those who control money. The quest for financing is no longer limited to relatively short periods of active campaigning. It goes on all the time. I know several members of Congress. They are, as far as I am aware, honest men. Some were wealthy before they entered politics. The rest live relatively modest lives, struggling with the financial concerns common to fairly well-paid middle-class citizens. All of them complain that they must spend about half of all their time—a portion of every week of every year—raising money: holding small parties, organizing dinners, paying private calls on individual contributors. These are men the people have entrusted with the governance of the nation. Yet less than half their time is available for the study of public issues and pending legislation. The frenetic pace of political life allows little margin for the creativity that comes from thoughtful meditation or reading.

As recently as a few decades ago, it was not thought that money would become the essential fuel of the political process, that the financing of campaigns would be the established foundation of politics. Yet this has happened. And it is a disaster. Wealth, and not the popular will, plays the largest role in determining who will be elected. It is the continued flow of money to officials who have fulfilled the expectations of the rich that has made it virtually impossible to defeat an incumbent.

In 1988, for example, more than $2.7 billion was spent on election campaigns, about two thirds of it in contests for Congress and the presidency. This was a 50 percent increase over the amount spent four years earlier. And the figure does not include about $43 million collected to help presidential candidates but not directly donated to their campaigns. It also does not include spending by the political action committees that were established by some candidates, an omission from the records that makes the real total unknowable.

These are numbers compiled by official and semi-official institutions. I have participated in several campaigns at the federal level, and I know there are many ways to make unrecorded and uncounted contributions—from extending "loans" destined for future cancellation, to the simple transfer of cash in an envelope or a briefcase, to more esoteric manipulations which, even if I understood them, would require a great amount of exposition. If we assume that the level of such illegal contributions did not rise significantly (a dubious assumption considering the rising value of political influence), we can estimate with some certainty that politicians spent at least $3 billion seeking election to offices of limited tenure, jobs that pay far less than executive jobs in even middle-sized corporations.

Why do candidates and campaigns (for it is not only the candidate who has a stake in the outcome of an election) spend so much? Usually it is because their opponents do. Sometimes it is just because they have the money. Politicians know that money influences the result of elections. They have come to believe that the more money they spend, the greater their chances of election. Once this is accepted, there is no reason for a candidate to limit spending. The only limit, therefore, is the amount he or she can raise.

Common sense tells us that most of the $3 billion spent in 1988 did not come from the average middle-class American; nor does the money that finances campaigns for other important offices—governorships and other unusually powerful state posts. It is "given" by individuals of great wealth, or by businesses—which, whatever the formal limits on contributions, can circumvent restrictions in a variety of ways. (For example, contributions can be funneled through family members and employees.) Since the rich are the only source of the large amounts of money used to finance political campaigns, their help must be solicited. And both they and the candidate know that a favorable response has a price. There is no misunderstanding. Moreover, nearly all candidates know that this year's election will probably not be their last. Even as the final results are posted, the search for money must be renewed. And it would be a foolish politician indeed who, once elected, cut himself off from previous contributors by refusing "perfectly reasonable" requests.

Some contributors are motivated by sincere ideological belief or personal attachment to a particular candidate. But they are a small minority. Most of the billions spent on elections are an investment. The "givers" are investing in access and influence, in the right to persuade or coerce an elected official to their point of view or to enlist his or her support in a dispute with regulatory officials. Most large businesses (and many small ones) are seriously affected by government—by the contours of legislation and, even more often, by the powers of the many agencies mandated to regulate various components of the economy. Effective influence over elected officials, who pass the laws and control the agencies, can shape the conduct of their business, open up opportunities or foreclose them, and—most important— influence their earnings and profits.

The relationship between business self-interest and campaign contributions is self-evident. Contributing to a campaign is a business transaction. And for both sides there is a bottom line. For the politician it is measured in votes. For the businessman the bottom line is potential profit, the protection of future earnings from adverse public action, and influence over elected officials. No sensible businessman would deny himself so potentially profitable an investment, especially since experience demonstrates that you get what you pay for. No senator or representative turns a large contributor away from his or her office door. If legitimate help—that is, assistance within the law—is wanted, it will be provided. A public servant is obliged, after all, to help constituents. And if the supplicant happens to come from another state, well, we're all Americans, aren't we?

Of course an elected official has many constituents who need help. And many receive it. But there is not time for everyone. It is a question of priorities. And somehow the highest priority always goes to the man with the money. The large contributor, or his representative, always receives respectful attention to his arguments, a sympathetic response, if not always a commitment to a request for an amendment to a pending bill, or shared indignation at mistreatment by some "idiot bureaucrat," perhaps followed by a call from the politician's office just to make sure the agency gives the contributor a fair hearing—and maybe more.

Influence on this scale is self-evident. But there is more, much more. "Influence" is an elusive word with subtle resonance. Under propitious circumstances, a barely perceptible shift, a slightly increased exertion of force, can transform influence into domination or even control. In many cases, the rising demand for money has already created the necessary circumstances and the shift has already occurred, transforming the structure of democratic capitalism.

For, most ominous and dangerous of all, the rising supremacy of money has seriously damaged the process of democracy, subjecting it to the rule of faction. Money stands athwart efforts to remodel the capitalist structure—to increase productivity and rebuild our stricken financial structure—because every change, no matter how beneficial it may ultimately prove to business, appears as a threat to some existing enterprise whose interests are already firmly rooted in the political structure. Franklin Delano Roosevelt once said that his principal task was to keep the bankers from committing suicide. The leaders of banking opposed his every measure. Supported by a stricken nation, he overcame their opposition. New laws were passed and stringent regulations imposed. And the banks finally prospered.

Earlier Herbert Hoover had supported banking reform. But the opposition of the banks defeated all reform legislation. According to historian Harris Warren, "They had not yet been whipped, shamed, exposed, and bankrupted into submission to reform demands." The banks won the battle in Congress, but it was a Pyrrhic victory. There ensued an average of 120 bank failures a month for forty-eight months in succession.

In 1910, *Bankers* magazine, with subdued exuberance, announced its discovery that "theoretically, the ballot con-

trols everything; but the spirit of political organization
. . . outside of legislative enactment now goes far to control
the ballot. Industrial and commercial organization, when it
desires to control the government, either Federal or State,
finds a political organization ready for its uses. The productive forces are the purse bearers. . . . They . . . furnish the
means by which the political organization which produces
the government is created and becomes effective. . . . More
and more the legislatures and executive powers of the Government are compelled to listen to the demands of organized business interests. That they are not entirely controlled by these interests is due to the fact that business
organization has not reached full perfection."

Although today business organization still falls short of
perfection, it has made a lot of progress. But progress has its
price. For today the power of wealth over our political system is far more extensive than the power that Roosevelt
confronted, and it will, unless eliminated, obstruct every
effort to modify the structure of free enterprise so as to
restore significant economic growth and enlarge every individual's opportunity to improve his or her standard of living.

After the Second World War, we were gifted with political
leaders possessed of firm convictions and—within the limits
of political reality—steadfast in their pursuit of principle.
Naturally we think of the men who occupied the White
House from the death of Roosevelt to the murder of John
F. Kennedy. But among its leaders, Congress also had men
of great ability and firm belief, willing to stand against the
shifting views of their colleagues, their party, and the public.
There were Midwesterners Robert Taft and Arthur Vandenberg; Southern senators Richard Russell and William
Fulbright; Wayne Morse from the Far West; and Eastern-
ers like Margaret Chase Smith, George Aiken, and Robert

Kennedy. One could add several names to this list. The number or selection is unimportant. What matters is that we had a wealth of leadership that ensured that public life would be a forum of debate to resolve the great issues of the day, from the Marshall Plan to Medicare to civil rights. Although many disagreed with the measures taken by government, few ascribed them to venality, opportunism, or indifference to the nation's welfare.

We still have officials of such high principle and purpose. But they are exceptions, and they have little influence over our political structure. The constitutionally appointed guardians of democratic sovereignty have fallen under the influence, even the command, of the very economic interests, and the concentrations of wealth and power, that they are empowered and mandated to regulate in service to our common well-being.

A leading member of the Senate recently observed that "Congress is in a total gridlock." He meant that the legislative and executive branches are unable, or unwilling, either to take any significant action to heal the endemic ills of society or even to remedy the more obvious deficiencies of government itself. Similar laments have come from other frustrated members of Congress. (And it takes a lot to disillusion a politician.) But none of them adds the obvious truth—which they all understand—that any substantial measures of reform would be opposed, and probably defeated, by already powerful and established interests. For any significant change, even those designed to increase prosperity and economic growth, always threatens, or appears to threaten, those who are prospering within the existing order—even if that order is one of national dissolution, decay and decline. (The introduction of the automobile, for example, led to the collapse of the horse-and-buggy industry. However, the leaders of that industry had no powerful lobby in Washington to provide government with arguments against crowding our roadways with dangerous and noisy machines, which their experts had proven would eventually require the taxpayer to finance a costly reconstruction of the streets.)

Not long ago, newspapers and television broadcasts described, somewhat breathlessly, what appeared to be a fierce debate over the substance of a "deficit reduction package." Its enactment, all our leaders agreed, was one of our highest national priorities. Democratic leaders proffered programs; Republicans responded with counterproposals. Network television showed us high officials hustling with solemn intensity from limousine to meeting. "Live" interviews were conducted with congressional leaders standing before the portals of government buildings or in offices where agitated aides moved through the camera's view. It all seemed quite animated, almost exciting.

This official drama deepened when President Bush personally convened leaders of both parties for a White House "summit" meeting (an evocative resonance of the old Cold War). Differences were reconciled and all parties finally emerged to inform an anxious nation that a final agreement had been reached. The result, applauded by leaders from both parties and swiftly enacted, was a program that has not prevented us from actually increasing our deficit, expanding the national debt, and increasing the annual interest on that debt to more than $300 billion a year—a drain on public funds that is growing twice as fast as the national economy.

Since no important private interest was to be damaged, and since neither party was willing to increase revenues or to agree on spending cuts, this outcome was probably inevitable. There is no other way to reduce deficits. The debate and the resulting "reduction package" were a charade—one that will greatly increase the burden on future generations.

But it did give political leaders an opportunity to tell their constituents they supported both the President and economy in government. And no important private interest had the slightest reason for concern.

Yet government is not a charade, nor do its officers lack purpose. Their appearance of futility helps mask the abandonment of their duty to the American community for service to private power.

Aware of the danger that factions (now called special economic interests) might seek dominating privilege, America's founders intended that representative democracy would be the community's protection. "To secure the public good and private rights against the danger of . . . faction," Madison wrote in the *Federalist Papers,* "is then the great object to which our inquiries are directed." "By a faction," Madison explained, "I understand a number of citizens . . . who are united and actuated by some common impulse of passion, or of interest, adverse to the rights of other citizens, or to the permanent and aggregate interests of the community. . . . Justice is the end of government. It is the end of civil society. It has ever been and ever will be pursued until it be obtained, or, until liberty is lost in the pursuit. In a society under which the stronger faction can readily unite and oppress the weaker, anarchy may as truly be said to reign as in a state of nature."

Our constitutional institutions were carefully contrived to protect against such oppression. Government, constrained only by the people's judgment in frequent elections, was given the constitutional mandate and the authority to protect our citizens against the "anarchy" that results when the weak are at the mercy of the strong. And these institutions have served this purpose more effectively and for a longer time than its framers could have imagined.

But the founders were not innocents. They understood that no institutions, and no system of institutions—unless supported and directed by the spirit and will of a free people—could ensure the common interest against the desires and purpose of powerful interests. Madison expressed their hope "that the public voice, pronounced by representatives of the people, will be . . . consonant to the public good." Yet he also warned that "the effect may be inverted, and Men of factious tempers, or local prejudices, or of sinister designs, may . . . first obtain the suffrages, and, then betray the interests of the people."

In our time, Madison's warning appears as prophecy. Today's institutions of representative democracy are a flimsy barrier, easily breached. Representatives of the people have themselves become willing servants of the strongest elements in civil society. And that shameful combination is contributing to the manifold afflictions of our citizens and to the decrease of American greatness.

Subservience to privilege is not bounded by party lines. Paying rhetorical lip service to the most urgent needs of the middle class and the poor, while refusing to take any constructive action to meet those needs, Republicans and Democrats alike—with several honorable exceptions—have husbanded the interests of the same masters. Always ready to rush to the aid of privilege, the masters of political Washington refuse even to confront the great issues of the day—the decay of the American standard of life, the deterioration of our society, the unjust and economically dangerous maldistribution of income, the dissolution of opportunity for millions, the destruction of nature for the sake of profit, the pillaging of the middle class to enrich the privileged, and, above all, the corruption of our political system. Thus, the solemn convocations within the historic chambers of Congress, and the sober assembly of high officials seated in carefully prescribed order around the octagonal Cabinet table, are merely an imposing show of orderly rule that masks the anarchy of which Madison warned.

The American people know this to be true. Almost every campaign demonstrates that politicians persistently underestimate the intelligence and instincts of the citizens, who are, by now, fully aware that most political rhetoric is meaningless and unmeant. They no longer look toward government for solution of the country's problems and believe, rightly, that party labels no longer reflect serious differences of ideology or conviction. If this is true—and it is more a fact than a rhetorical accusation—then why should people engage their energies and emotions in the political process? Why should they even vote, knowing that, whatever the outcome, nothing will change: The poor will remain poor; jobs will be insecure or hard to find; times will be tough; oil will befoul the air and—occasionally but inevitably— devastate the oceans?

The rise of faction has been assisted (though somewhat marginally) by the bewildering complexities of many issues that confront the Congress. For unlike the general public, and unlike many representatives, the emissaries appointed by faction to represent them in Washington know exactly what is being drafted and debated. Few citizens and few members of Congress, for example, understand the complexities of banking laws, the intricacies of securities regulation, the labyrinthine chambers of the tax code. As a result, legislation on such subjects is formulated, and its fate is often determined, by small committees dominated by a few men or even a single individual. Their power over legislation that affects a multitude of interests in many parts of the country influences other legislators to support their recommendations. Thus, they not only write laws; they can often pass them.

And it is far easier for "factions" to reach and influence a few men, or a single man, than to suborn the entire Congress. Indeed, the representatives of affected private institutions can readily develop working relationships with key committee members, and help raise funds for campaigns. They are often drawn upon to provide "information" to our elected officials. They understand the law; they can explain it; they supply an abundance of "expert" studies and statistics. Personal relationships, access to information, intelligent understanding of even the most esoteric provisions in a proposed law (and an often undisclosed awareness of its possible benefits) often translate into influence. And influence, if it extends to the right people, is power. For example, probably not a half-dozen members of Congress understood the implications of the law that allowed thrift institutions to make high-risk investments and, at the same time, raised government insurance of deposits to $100,000. Acting on the assurances of the House committee and its chairman—whose profitable subservience to the banking industry was notorious—the House of Representatives readily enacted the legislation, which was to cost the taxpayers untold billions of dollars.

For about a year, Congress has been considering bills to "reform" the banking system, whose only real purpose—concealed beneath multitudinous pages of technical text—is to increase the power and increase the permitted activities of the country's banks. Given our recent experience with the skill and prudential wisdom of our financial institutions one could scarcely conceive of more foolish and economically dangerous measures. But such a bill might pass anyway. Few can understand it, but everyone favors reform. And the banks have flooded the chambers of Congress with experts anxious to explain the benefits to the nation. (And even this lobbying is merely intended to provide members with politically acceptable reasons for their support of powerful committee chairmen. As one junior congressman remarked, "When you go into the committee room to draft a bill, it is already too late. Any significant amendment is quickly discarded. The deal has already been cut." And who cut the deal?)

And who, I wonder, understood the mammoth Tax Reform Act of 1986, with which "liberal" Democrats assumed the leadership in a successful legislative effort to reduce taxes on the rich, move us toward increasing the tax burden on working Americans, and deprive us of resources necessary to help meet traditional liberal concerns? Almost no one among those who prepared the legislation and led it toward enactment. And no one at all foresaw its implications for the future—except, of course, for the highly paid tax experts retained to testify by those interests that would be enriched, or a few economists whose warnings probably never got past some assistant's desk.

Because congressional issues are so varied and complex, and because members of Congress spend a great deal of time raising money and cultivating constituents for the next election, most elected officials feel compelled to rely on hired staff for analysis and judgment. In recent years those staffs have swollen to monstrous proportions, enveloping nearly every individual member of Congress and every major committee. Indeed, representatives no longer have staffs. They have bureaucracies. They engage, at public expense, armies of men and women—mostly young—whose studied knowledge of pending legislation gives them a great deal of power to influence their employer's vote; they also share offices with those other staff members whose principal function is to assure the reelection of their boss. Through these aides the requirements of politics—especially the essential help from powerful business and financial institutions—yield still further access to the mind of the legislator. There are not many with the resources—lawyers and lobbyists—even to discover which staff members are responsible for which bill.

However, the complexity of issues is not an especially important cause of the increasing power of factions. It merely eases the exercise of power they already possess. Much past legislation—especially that of the New Deal and the Great Society—was equally complicated. Elaborately intricate policies were enacted. New institutions with large responsibilities were established. Without the need of help from large staffs, these bills were debated at a level of understanding and intelligence at least equal to that now displayed. They were often amended in ways that proved them to be clearly understood. And many of them—not all—effectively contributed to the growth of national abundance and an improving standard of life for millions of citizens.

The dominant cause of the deterioration and virtual paralysis in political leadership, its subservience to those who control wealthy private institutions, remains the soaring power of money within the political process. There is no more dramatic illustration of the triumph of private economic power than the scandals of the past decade, abuses of such monumental proportion they make Teapot Dome look like a robbery of the corner grocery store. In little more than ten years more than a trillion dollars has been stolen from the American taxpayers. Scandals were heaped so rapidly one upon the other that we barely had time to reflect on one revelation of corruption before the next was upon us. We have already almost forgotten the "military procurement" scandal—the $1,000 hammers and the $900 toilet seat, which themselves were merely easily dramatized token illustrations of the huge amounts of money skimmed and diverted from the military program by industries and some of our most prestigious universities. Yet there have been no indictments, no trials, no convictions.

Only a few years ago we discovered that the Department of Housing and Urban Development—a Cabinet department established to assist the ordinary citizen and the poor—was handing out contracts to politically and personally favored contractors, without regard to cost and without requiring bids. Public money went into private pockets without regard for the general welfare. And there have been no indictments, no trials, no convictions.

More recently we have experienced the so-called savings-and-loan scandal, which may ultimately cost us close to a trillion dollars. Urged on by a handful of wealthy and generous "contributors," Congress passed laws that allowed savings-and-loan chieftains to use money entrusted to them by depositors to make extraordinarily risky investments—investments that no sound, conservatively managed thrift would consider, and that had previously been prohibited. As an added incentive, Congress also increased government insurance of deposits. Meanwhile, the so-called regulators of the national banking system were encouraged, stimulated, and occasionally coerced into giving banking executives free rein. No investment—no resort in the desert or loan to the almost bankrupt—was too risky. Most of the transactions that led to disaster were approved—directly or in silent acquiescence—by government officers responsible for ensuring the soundness of the thrifts and protecting their depositors. When the illusion dissolved, when the "thrift" institutions began to collapse, someone had to pay. Not the miscreants. Not their collaborators in politics. Not the "regulators" who failed their public trust. But, since the lost deposits were federally insured, it is the taxpayers—you and I, and, ultimately, our children—who will pay.

In earlier periods, scandals of much lesser proportion

evoked an outpouring of public wrath. Congress was propelled into detailed investigations. Ambitious prosecutors were sent to subpoena and examine books and files. Heads rolled. Entire administrations were discredited. President Dwight D. Eisenhower was forced to fire his valued chief of staff because he had accepted the gift of a vicuña coat from an inconsequential businessman. Harding's attorney general was indicted. Grant's presidency was fatally tainted by his subordinates' misuse of public lands and Indian trading posts.

The very different reaction to the scandals of the 1980s discloses a widespread disillusionment, almost a public acceptance that corruption is inevitable, that government can no longer be relied upon as a barrier to those who would augment their fortunes at the people's expense. There is a great deal of justification for this lack of faith, but not for a belief that the situation is irremediable. The rascals may be firmly ensconced, but the people who put them there can remove them.

Government's own failure to react, except for some expressions of indignation and a few token and inconclusive hearings, does not flow from an excess of charity or forgiveness. It is a result of the fact that many in Congress and the executive were implicated. It was Congress that passed, and a President who signed, the sloppy, ill-conceived laws that removed the barriers to larceny by financial institutions. They unlocked the vault. It was federal regulators, employees of the public, hired by the executive and dependent upon the Congress, who abdicated their responsibility to enforce standards of conduct designed to protect the public. Their bad judgment resulted from a fairly low level of competence; from often intense and recurrent pressures from powerful members of Congress who had received large campaign contributions from prospering bankers; and from the general temper of an age when it seemed the fields of finance and enterprise were heaped with gold.

The young Abraham Lincoln described politicians as "a set of men who have interests aside from the interests of the people, and who, to say the most of them, are, taken as a mass, at least one long step removed from honest men. I say this with greater freedom because, being a politician myself, none can regard it as personal." But Lincoln was only twenty-eight years old when he said this to the Illinois legislature, and his experience had been confined to the political figures of frontier America. Moreover, through the long career that followed, Lincoln himself was to prove an honest man; and so were many of the political leaders I have known.

I know of no conclusive evidence that any elected official involved in the abuses of our time was personally dishonest (naturally, campaign contributions were always acceptable), although several were on the edge. And we can be certain that the future will yet bring some disagreeable revelation. It is difficult to believe that, in an age when a few people were permitted to make a great deal of money at the public's expense, no official yielded to the temptations of greed. It was in the air. Possibly, with little or no awareness of danger or larcenous intent, politicians just went along with the desires and requests of the interests to which the political process has submitted its authority. It is also possible that some shared more directly in the spoils of private privilege.

Yet who will sit in judgment when the judges themselves must stand among the accused? There can be no absolution for a government so totally derelict. Businessmen and financiers throughout the country knew what was happening—in banking, in housing, in military spending. Yet no member of Congress, no leader, initiated, or even demanded, an investigation until it was too late—further evidence of the debilitating submission of public power to private interest, to factions.

There is no need to accumulate evidence to demonstrate the failures of government—the virtual paralysis of public action and the mediocrity that pervades our political dialogue and public action. It is almost as if government had become a kind of public-relations game in which it is enough to name problems and call for their resolution without any need to act. "We must improve our schools," says the President. "We must preserve our environment and reduce our deficit," say the leaders of Congress. And, presto, children learn, nature is restored, and the deficit disappears.

But government is not a game. It is leading us into a depression that will undermine the source of American greatness—not our wealth of military strength, but the liberty that we created amid a world of despotisms and sustained for two centuries, the liberty that, in Lincoln's words, "gave promise that in due time the weights should be lifted from the shoulders of all men."

Every poll, every "in-depth" survey, reflects increasing public disenchantment with politics. But no political scientist is needed to confirm what the conversations of daily life so clearly reveal: Many, perhaps most, Americans are aware that government is under the sway of privilege, that it lacks the will and intention to resolve the problems that are gradually diminishing the standard of American life. This disenchantment is there because the harsh winds of experience have blown enchantment away.

The citizenry's frequently cited "apathy" toward politics and elections is a natural consequence of this truth. Americans understand that no matter who wins an election, the lobbyists for wealth and privilege, the Washington emissaries of large business and organized economic interests, will remain in control. Indeed, in our time, corruption has insinuated itself so thoroughly that resignation seems to have displaced protest, arousing the apprehension that today's rule of faction may not be an episode, but the beginning of a transformation in our democracy.

America has experienced other moments in which private power has dominated public life. But we have always found the strength to mount effective opposition and a struggle for correction. For example, the Populist movement and the Progressive movement confronted immense and powerful factions, dominant concentrations of wealth and power. And though incomplete, Populist and Progressive success helped restore the country and its government to the people. Though it is still inchoate and unfocused, we have the same power they did: the right to rule, the sovereignty, inscribed in the Constitution and ratified by history.

In order to recapture government and liberate it from the rule of faction, it will be necessary to make changes in the structure of political life, as we have done many times before. One does not need a litany of illustrative examples to understand that today's political institutions are far different from those that governed the land of Jefferson and Madison. To be sure, many of the names are the same. But the dimensions and distribution of power among these public bodies, and between government and the people, has been altered, not once but many times, and not in minor or trivial aspects but in the essential structure of democratic government. And many of these changes were in response to the problems and opportunities of a changing American economy. For example, the turn-of-the-century demand for the direct election of senators was largely a response to the Senate's refusal to act against the "trusts" that had become the dominant institutions of economic life, and whose

42

power was thought to threaten the very existence of a competitive marketplace. (In the 1890s, John D. Rockefeller controlled 80 percent of America's oil production.) Other changes, more ominous for democracy, like the contemporary transition to an imperial presidency, were a consequence of the natural tendency of power to aggrandize itself, even at the expense of constitutional principles. But in politics as in economics, the willingness to make fundamental change has been part of the American tradition and a source of our ability to endure and to grow.

RECAPTURING DEMOCRACY

Restoring the institutions of democracy to the service of the people is among the highest priorities of any movement for democratic capitalism. The suggestions that follow are intended as a start toward that end, and a beginning point for realistic debate about remedies for a corrupt and ineffectual system that no longer serves the welfare of the nation or the intentions of the founders.

A very substantial reduction in campaign spending and, consequently, in the need for contributions will, in a single stroke, drastically diminish the power of wealth to corrupt the political process. More than any other single act, it will restore us to the established traditions of democratic rule. Wealth and business will still have a great deal of influence, but their ability to displace the sovereignty of the people will be dissipated. Therefore, we should reduce both individual campaign contributions and total campaign expenditures to a small fraction of their present level. There is no sign that spending a lot of money improves the quality of elected leadership. Quite the contrary. We are spending far more and getting much less, by any measure of intelligence, leadership, or courage. If all candidates are subject to equal limits, if the playing field is relatively even, then we can trust the people to choose. They may not always make the best choice. But that is what democracy is all about. And we can be certain—as recent experience proves—that lavish spending does not lessen the chances for error.

The complete achievement of this objective may require amending the Constitution, since the Supreme Court has ruled that an individual, protected by the right of free speech, may spend unlimited amounts of his own money. However, our national army of infinitely ingenious lawyers can almost certainly find ways to limit this egregiously unfair advantage for the wealthy, perhaps by conditioning any public financing on a commensurate reduction of individual spending.

Television stations should be required to give free and equal time to all office-seekers qualified for election under state law. This would give voters a chance to see and judge all candidates for public office. The purchase of television time is now the single most expensive cost of campaigning. It is also the only effective means of mass communication. Substantial reductions in spending limits should neither prevent candidates from presenting their principles and programs nor deprive voters of the chance to make an informed judgment. To the dismay of many, television has become the most critical component in a political campaign, and an indispensable part of the democratic process. It has an obligation to that process and to the people, who own the airwaves and have loaned them to broadcasters—a loan that has brought immense profits to many. Certainly television stations and networks have no moral standing (or, one hopes, any desire) to object if a limited amount of time must be given to candidates for office. In so doing—even under the duress of law—they would be helping to enlighten the public, and, equally important, making it far more feasible to reduce the importance of money to the conduct of democracy.

We should restrict the often incestuous relationship between government agencies and the very industries they regulate. Few of those who direct administrative agencies have any contact with their true constituencies: those segments of the general public they are commanded to protect against business abuse. However, they frequently meet—officially and socially—with leaders of the businesses they regulate. These relationships obviously provide another conduit for exercise of private power over the conduct of government, and their use for that purpose has been amply documented.

Over decades, teams of objective experts, many assembled at presidential request, have submitted reports proving that administrative agencies often act to benefit the subjects of their regulation, to the detriment of the general interest they were established to serve and sometimes to the extent of violating the very statutes that established them. As a result of these reports, and an occasional public scandal, agencies have been censured, changes have been proposed, new forms of legislation drafted. But almost nothing has been done. And the agencies have remained a primary source of the influence exercised by special interests—by factions—over the democratic process. Many agencies have served the country well, of course. Many regulators are unimpeachably committed to their public responsibilities. But the exceptions are large and frequent enough to require corrective action.

The principal blame for the defects of regulatory agencies lies with Congress, which, by providing broad general mandates and leaving the content of more specific rules of business conduct to appointed administrators, has, in practical effect, abdicated its legislative power to individuals who are neither elected by nor directly accountable to the people. The Congress should be required, therefore, at a minimum, to ratify all administrative regulations in an effort to ensure that the mandate imposed by general legislation is being enforced and, more than incidentally, to make itself directly accountable for some of the most important actions of those agencies it created and which it finances.

In the long run, neither Congress nor the executive is a match for an ensconced bureaucracy whose employees— even when attacked—are fully prepared to temporarily mend their ways while awaiting a change of political power and control. Ultimately, bureaucrats' power comes from their longevity. Important economic decisions are made by regulators who can expect to outlast elected Presidents and representatives, and whose understanding of regulated industries comes to exceed that of those who established them in office and of the congressional committees that oversee them. But the constitutional design never embraced the establishment of a semipermanent and powerful bureaucracy relatively free of the restraints of representative democracy. "I am for responsibilities at short periods," said Jefferson, referring to the tenure of appointed public officials. Therefore, we should establish a fixed term for all administrative agencies and most Cabinet departments. At the end of that term, perhaps around twenty years, the enabling legislation would expire, requiring Congress to redebate and reconsider the wisdom and practical effect of laws passed to meet the needs of a previous generation. This alone would exert a powerful chilling effect on the bureaucracy and restore at least some elements of democratic authority over those who possess such significant authority over the conduct of national affairs.

Jefferson once suggested that democracy could best be preserved by having a revolution every twenty years. He was not talking about administrative agencies or Cabinet departments in particular. And while history has made it impracticable, and probably undesirable, to overthrow entire governments at periodic intervals, the considerations that supported his belief apply with special force to agencies and departments relatively immune from the changing popular will. By requiring Congress to reaffirm or amend the conduct of established bureaucracy, we would strengthen democratic control over the dangerous alliance between special interests and an entrenched bureaucracy.

Congressional staffs should be greatly reduced. They do not appear to have enhanced the wisdom of our legislature or its capacity to deal with national problems. Instead, they have given elected officials an opportunity to reduce their personal responsibility to understand and to judge the laws that shape national affairs, while providing an additional conduit for the influence of factions. Few realize that when they elect an individual to Congress, they have also chosen a platoon of assistants whose views and capacities, though totally unknown to the voter, will significantly influence the conduct of the legislative branch. The principle which asserts that work expands to fill the available time is more a truism than a jest. Similarly, our elected officials will increase the number of their employees to the limit of their budget. And since they also control that budget, they have been able to expand their staffs to numbers larger than those previously required by the presidential office itself. Roosevelt managed to steer us through a depression and a world war with fewer assistants than are now employed by any committee chairman in Congress. And few would argue that the result has been an improvement in the quality of government.

Members of Congress and executive departments should be required to make all contacts with lobbyists or other representatives of private interests a matter of public record. Such communication cannot be prevented. Indeed, it would be undesirable to do so. But certainly the public's right to know extends to communications between elected representatives or appointed officials and the emissaries of private businesses and organizations. At the very least, compulsory public disclosure might act as a salutary restraint.

Limits should be imposed on the number of consecutive terms to be served by members of Congress. Few measures are more likely to strengthen democratic control. The architects of our democracy did not contemplate the growth of a professional political class whose entire careers would be devoted to the acquisition and exercise of public authority. It was, rather, envisioned that public-spirited individuals would depart their customary occupations for relatively short periods of public service, thus encouraging citizens of integrity and experience to share in governing the nation. Madison believed that the most effective guarantee of a government committed to pursue the public good would be "the restraint of frequent elections," a restraint that is nullified by the ability of an incumbent to retain his office for long years.

Regardless of the quality of his service to the country, an incumbent, especially one whose seniority has brought him power and a substantial flow of campaign funds, has a substantial advantage over any challenger. Yet after a long period of service, with reelection fairly secure, a member of Congress becomes more concerned with the internecine struggles and the limited horizons of the Capitol than with the rapidly shifting conditions of the nation. Jefferson wrote that there was "neither reason nor safety in making the public functionaries independent of the nation for life or even for a long period of years." He was explaining his refusal to seek election to a third term. (Washington's earlier decision to retire at the end of two terms had not yet attained the status of a precedent.) But Jefferson's reasoning reflected his belief that no one should hold public power for a long period of years. This conviction was given the force of law when the Constitution was amended to limit a President to two terms.

Congress, however, is exempt from the limits imposed on presidential tenure. Indeed, the increased importance of money to finance campaigns has enormously enhanced the probabilities of reelection. Contributors find it far more advantageous to funnel money toward incumbents whose power is already established, whose views are known, and whose relationship with business is established. The result has been the sustained tenure of officials who must continually cultivate the sources of reelection while neglecting larger concerns. Since it is extremely difficult to oust an incumbent, many professional politicians are able to accumulate inordinate power simply by virtue of their long tenure in office, regardless of their competence or conviction. Though they nominally represent particular constituencies, their authority is extended to political domination over matters of significance to the entire nation, and they thus provide a readily identifiable focus for private interests seeking to assert their will.

Recently elected members of Congress, even if gifted with substantial talent, are forced to waste their abilities, because real authority—the ability to act—is closely held by those who have been in office for many years. Their independence of action is impaired; their convictions are accommodated to the needs and wishes of the congressional colleagues upon whom they depend for choice committee assignments and steady advance through the hierarchy of congressional power. Their professional lives are centered, not upon the afflictions of the country, but in the incestuous world of Washington, where it is essential to abandon maverick tendencies for the more politically advantageous willingness to "get along" with one's leaders, and to compromise one's views, not out of political necessity, but to win and retain the favor of one's fellow politicians. The result is to intensify an unwillingness to defy committee chairmen, the party leadership, and the views of their colleagues. Members of Congress often surrender their own views to the chairmen of their committees, individuals who have acquired large power not because they possess superior ability or wisdom or expertise, but merely because they have managed to stay in office for many years.

A long continuation in office, carrying with it the enormous electoral advantage of incumbency, also obstructs the entrance of new individuals whose experience and interests have developed outside politics, and who, coming from a variety of occupations and experience, might bring some much-needed creativity and imagination to Washington. Limitations on consecutive terms, of course, would result in the departure of some individuals who have served the nation well. But if we have found it advantageous to limit the terms of Presidents—whose duties are the most complex and onerous of all—then the country can survive the departure of those few members of Congress who have earned a right to the public's trust. And the compensating advantages would be enormous: a serious reduction in the power of money to influence the political process; the removal of many who—despite their lack of qualifications—are able to retain office because of the considerable advantages conferred by the mere fact of incumbency; and the encouragement of capable individuals who are now unwilling to abandon their present occupations to enter the political profession against the opposition of powerful incumbents. "I see the best effects produced," Jefferson explained, "by sending our young statesmen to Congress. They see the affairs of the confederacy from a high ground; they learn the importance of the union, and befriend federal measures when they return."

The problem is that they don't return. Instead they stay in Washington, submitting themselves to the authority of the congressional bureaucracy and the power of those whose favor is helpful—often essential—to continued tenure. Increasingly, it is not the people who rule Washington. Washington rules Washington. The continual infusion of individuals with varied knowledge and experience, free from dependence on both the political hierarchy and private power, able to speak and vote their convictions without fear of career-threatening public opposition, would be a large and significant step toward strengthening the authority of democracy.

In the 1840s, Abraham Lincoln lost his seat in Congress, largely because of his fierce opposition to our war with Mexico. He was aware that his unpopular position would probably end his tenure. But there was always his law practice in Illinois, an occupation he preferred to indulging the political expedient of abandoning a deeply held conviction. Lincoln was to go on to greater things, in part because he had learned that compromise has its limits, that public office is not worth accommodating firmly rooted beliefs to the transient vagaries of public opinion. Those lessons were to serve the nation well. Limiting terms will not give us a government of Lincolns. It will, however, increase the number of those willing to act upon those convictions that a democratic constituency has chosen them to pursue.

Our political structure has become corrupted and has been rendered impotent to restore a declining America.

Democracy bestows on the sovereign people the means and the obligation to alter or abolish misdirected or abusive power. Only by acting toward this end can we sustain our loyalty to two hundred years of history and help preserve America's defining values for our descendants. Our duty is thus clearly established. Only our will is in doubt. But should we withdraw from this effort, then we will have also abandoned our essential loyalty to the great experiment that is America.

III

The Betrayal of Democratic Capitalism

AN ECONOMY is not a statistical abstraction. Properly understood, it is the way 250 million Americans expend most of their energies, seek personal fulfillment in their work and through the rewards of that work, and struggle to sustain the bonds of family and community. It tells us what we value and what we will strive to attain. Thus, our economy—any economy—reflects and partially determines both the human condition and human behavior. It is, therefore, no coincidence that our economic difficulties, the decline of income and opportunity, the widening divisions in our population, and the diminution of our ability to create wealth, have been accompanied by serious and growing defects in other aspects of American life: mounting violence and poverty, a failing educational system, the devastation of nature.

It is unnecessary to multiply the menacing symptoms of a continuing decline in the American promise. No barrage of official optimism, flag-waving, or commanding exhortations to patriotic belief can mask the truth. The American people already sense the onset, the suggestive stirring, of decline. Most have felt it brush against their daily lives or that of their neighbors, perhaps as lightly as a falling leaf with its intimation of a changing season. We listen to official reassurances, believe (though with less certainty than before) that government means well, and join in patriotic celebrations. Yet we can feel something in the air, perhaps only a sense of our own vulnerability, perhaps something stronger. The future no longer appears quite so secure, the reward for labor not quite so likely. Many see their fellow citizens in distress. Most feel that the country is no longer immune from serious failures, even collapse. We worry about providing for our children. We begin to fear that it may be necessary to abandon some of the ambitions we once held for the maturing child. And the more thoughtful among us wonder if our generation will be the first in two centuries to bequeath a diminished America.

In the American system of democratic capitalism, government and business are partners, two aspects of the same whole. But they are not equals, not in principle and not in law. Government is our instrument for expressing and enforcing the collective will of the people. It is commanded to guard the needs and principles of the entire American community against infringement by any combination of private wealth and power.

Government has abdicated this obligation, usually in order to benefit the more influential members of the private sector. By helping to strengthen special interests against the dangers of a free economy, government has in reality contributed to the continuing deterioration of American capitalism, and thus to our current decline. Under the shelter of public protections, special benefits, preferred treatment, unwillingness to enforce laws enacted to protect the public and liberate the market, much of American enterprise—with many large and proud exceptions—has become flabby, timid, less able to compete in our own marketplace and in the mushrooming marketplaces of the industrialized world.

A little more than twenty years ago, America was still the wealthiest and most productive nation on earth. In the years since the end of the Second World War, the average family income had doubled. Our capacity to create wealth was unequaled. Twenty-six percent of our work force was in manufacturing, only slightly less than the 28 percent Japan draws today from a much smaller pool of workers. We had a positive trade balance. Our production workers were the highest-paid in the world. And our productivity was growing over 3 percent a year. No other country—indeed, not even the entire industrial world combined—could match our pool of scientific talent, our capacity for innovation, our flow of invention and scientific advance. We had gone to the moon, and we had laid the groundwork for a series of technological revolutions in areas as disparate as electronics and plastics.

Of course, other nations—largely inspired by the golden prospect that American accomplishments had unveiled—entered the competitive marketplace. They brought energy, determination, and skill to the struggle. But no country was better or more abundantly endowed to meet the challenges they posed. And we could have done it. No one prohibited our automobile manufacturers from making better cars, more appropriately adapted to a changing marketplace. No "czar" of production instructed our steel industries to cling to obsolete modes of production and ignore the obvious improvements in modernization and efficiency being demonstrated in the middle of Europe and on the edge of Asia. No perverse genie of electromagnetism decreed that our huge electrical combines and centers of technological production should abandon television sets and camcorders or fail to improve the quality of refrigerators and ovens. And we had plenty of money to do it all—to modernize, innovate, produce, and compete. For we then commanded an immense pool of investment capital within a financial structure so desperate to loan money that it wantonly shipped off billions to the eternal oblivion of Peru and other nations of the Third World. The capital was there. And even conservative investors could be comforted by knowing that we were the largest creditor nation in the world, possibly in the history of the world.

No, the fault has not been in our stars, but in ourselves. And what a fall there has been. Since 1980, our economic growth has tumbled to its lowest rate since the Great Depression. The income of most American families is stagnant or declining. Wages of production workers have dropped from first to tenth in the industrialized world. Our growth in productivity has come to a standstill. In a single decade a trade surplus has been replaced by a $910 billion deficit. Total foreign investment in America has risen from $83 trillion ten years ago to about $400 trillion today. Our financial structure cannot meet our needs for capital investment. And we have the distinction of having become the largest debtor nation in the world, possibly in the history of the world. But most painful of all has been the erosion of economic opportunity, the chance to enrich the quality of one's life and bequeath even larger possibilities to one's children.

Where have all the promises gone? And where is America going, that land of dreams that seemed so close to becoming reality? The answer must come from us. And quickly. For the future may yield no chance to choose. Events and conditions can outrun even the swiftest and most determined.

In the last two decades the engine of American abundance has begun to falter. Our ability to create wealth is deteriorating, and its impairment is the principal cause of our present economic decline. We have neglected the supporting truths of successful capitalism, the most important of which is that we create wealth by making things. Individuals or businesses combine materials with labor to create a product that others will buy for more than the costs of creation. That difference measures the increase in wealth to the entrepreneur and to the economy as a whole, whether the work be undertaken by a gargantuan enterprise or by a single individual working in a makeshift shop in the family garage. Everything else— however important to a functioning economy—is tributary to the manufacturing process. A country gifted with the most cunning accountants and artful lawyers, brokers of unmatched proficiency, an army of wizardly mechanics schooled in the most intricate mysteries of technology, and bankers who were prodigies of finance, if it did not engage in manufacturing, would still be condemned to almost universal poverty. "Industry is the only lasting foundation of a nation's power," writes Jacques Attali in his illuminating and ominous book *Millennium,* "and it is in this sense that the signs of America's lasting decline are everywhere."

In almost every aspect of production—from steel to automobiles to chemicals—our share of the market (both domestic and overseas) is being steadily displaced by the vitality and ingenuity of others. In the past fifteen years we have lost 6 percent of our share in the world market, while Japan gained 15 percent. Lands and peoples we defeated or liberated during the Second World War have already outdistanced us in the production and sale of many consumer goods. They have surpassed us in industries ranging from high technology to basic materials. And in almost every aspect of production they are working, with considerable success, to achieve or increase a competitive advantage.

For example, America exports almost no automobiles or televisions or household appliances, although we buy an abundance of such products imported from foreign manufacturers. And in consumer electronics—an industry created largely by American inventions—the American share of the world market has collapsed from 70 percent in 1960 to an insignificant 4 percent today. With the important exception of microprocessors, not one significant civilian product that has appeared in the past few years was developed in the United States. Our share of the market for machine tools—a product essential to modern production, and a telling sign of a country's competitiveness—has fallen from 25 percent to 5 percent over the last thirty years. In that same period, Japan's share rose from 0 percent to 22 percent today. In all products that use modern high technology our deficit has increased sixfold, with the exception of computers and aerospace, where we still have a surplus. This aspect of decline is especially significant since products that incorporate technological advances will inevitably assume a larger role in all industrialized economies.

But there is no need to multiply evidence of our dwindling ability to sustain our once unchallenged economic preeminence. A brief stroll through rush-hour streets—crowded with cars from Japan and Europe—should provide all the evidence a skeptic might need. For further confirmation, simply turn on the television, listen to the stereo, warm a snack in the microwave—while first pausing for a glimpse at the brand labels that adorn these sleekly engineered amenities of technology, as a reminder that you are the willing, if unintentional, host to invaders from lands where American armies once marched.

Foreign businesses have coupled their American success with inroads into other markets. One cannot drive the streets of Rio or Nairobi without passing the myriad Toyotas, Nissans, and other foreign vehicles whose virtues are proclaimed from billboards at every major intersection. Nor will a visit to stores in the burgeoning markets of Asia reveal a large proportion of American goods among the products that crowd the increasingly well-stocked shelves of commerce.

Wealth is created in a competitive marketplace, where the success, even the survival, of private enterprises depends on a continual, unrelenting struggle to make products more desirable—better, cheaper, more closely adapted to the shifting needs and desires of consumers. And in the age of technology, successful competition also requires innovation—the modification of existing goods, the development of new products, the increase of efficiency and quality by transforming established methods of production and doing business.

Competition may be a threat to individual enterprises and those who own or control them. But it is today, as always, an essential stimulus to the creation of wealth. The ideological justifications for economic competition are not metaphysical, but functional. Competition vivifies the economy by rewarding superior performance: innovation, efficiency, energy. It is the instrument that can make the pursuit of self-interest advance the common interest.

That is why guarding the freedom of the market is among the most important obligations of democratic government. Indeed, this authority and responsibility is the defining attribute of democratic capitalism. Since the market must be both free and competitive, it is government's duty to prevent restraints on competition imposed by private business and to eliminate flaws in the structure of enterprise that diminish its ability to compete. When government enacts laws against monopoly, regulates the securities market, and builds the railroads, it is responding in different ways to the same obligation. And government's significant abandonment of that obligation is a major cause of our present decline.

Through most of our history, the competitive struggle that created our nation's wealth was largely confined to our own country. Now others have entered the arena. Our ability to maintain the American way of life will be seriously—perhaps decisively—affected by our success in overcoming competitive challenges from burgeoning economies on three continents. We are failing to meet this challenge, a failure that will, unless remedied, continue to undermine the quality of American life. Yet our once peerless industrial might is the means through which we create wealth. Our ability to innovate, to produce, to improve efficiency and productivity, thus enhancing our ability to compete, is our only means of increasing abundance, our only means of arresting deterioration.

Sometime during the Vietnam War, the seemingly infinite prospect of ever-mounting abundance began to dim. The change was imperceptible at first. Yet it has now become evident that during the 1970s our ability to create wealth began to slow. The rate of economic growth fell below that of the previous decade, dropped even further in the 1980s, and by the early 1990s had virtually evaporated, falling to an average of less than one half of one percent a year. It is the lowest rate of growth since the Great Depression. This decline in our ability to create wealth brought the long period of increasing personal abundance and a rising standard of living to an end. Over the last two decades the average family income has actually gone down for 80 percent of the American people, despite the increasing number of families in which two adults are working. Since the 1970s, and even during the false prosperity of the 1980s, the net worth of the average American family declined. It is now 4 percent less than it was in 1973. (By contrast, the wealth of the richest

20 percent of households increased about 14 percent during the same period. For them, prosperity was real.)

The dull statistics of change, dryly resistant to imaginative understanding, mask the realities of domestic hardship and tragedy. Many of those whose income is declining, whose future livelihood is uncertain, can no longer buy homes. Seventy-one percent of all families in which the chief breadwinner is under thirty-five cannot afford median-priced homes in their neighborhoods. Already-established householders now agonize over their ability to sustain the burden of mortgage payments. The average new car, once the proud emblem of entrance into middle-class America, now costs 47 percent of median annual family income—25 percent more than it did just a decade ago. Increasing numbers of hardworking citizens, willing to sacrifice their own desires, find it difficult, even impossible, to fulfill their dream of a college education for their children. Many must confront the specter of illness without means to secure the quality of medical care that is now reserved for the comparatively wealthy, or they postpone costly visits to doctors until the symptoms of disease are far advanced.

This current decline in income follows a rather long period of sustained growth. During the two and a half decades that followed the Second World War, average family income doubled. We became a middle-class nation. The onset of stagnation and decline was, consequently, made more severe because it was unexpected. People had lived, not just on their paychecks, but on the expectation that they would be promoted, their jobs upgraded, longevity rewarded, compensation raised—and that their investments would maintain or increase their value. Out of belief in the false promise of mounting prosperity, or simply to maintain their standard of living, Americans borrowed against an uncertain future.

Huge quantities of private debt—credit cards, automobile payments, mortgages—were incurred, all in anticipation that income would increase. (After all, the bankers sagely advised, "You can't go wrong with real estate.") As a result, by the late 1980s the average American's individual debt amounted to an unprecedented 66 percent of income. The burden of interest payments and the ultimate necessity to repay creditors were added to the individual's economic difficulties. When President Bush rather casually suggested that interest on credit cards be reduced from an outrageous and usurious 19.8 percent, the banks mounted a counterattack in the media and in Washington. The proposal was swiftly, almost apologetically, withdrawn. A naive President just didn't understand who was really in charge—or, more likely, he had a momentary lapse of memory. After all, why shouldn't an ordinary citizen be required to pay higher interest than unprofitable businesses, real estate speculators, or bankrupt foreign countries?

Those middle-class Americans who were fortunate to have received money in excess of their desire for consumption invested in the surest things of all. They invested in America. So money flowed into the securities of new or expanding enterprises, overvalued real estate, venture-capital funds, even junk bonds. And many have since seen hard-earned savings, sedulously put aside to protect their futures against the potential ravages of decline or advancing age, begin to dissolve. Their confidently constructed security is being displaced by fearful concern. Now they are forced to cut back. Not just because expectations have not been met. But out of a growing apprehension that their circumstances might continue to deteriorate. And that necessity to conserve reverberates throughout the economy.

Below the increasingly besieged middle class are the millions of Americans officially classified as poor, those whose annual income is less than $12,000 for a family of four, or $6,000 for individuals. In recent years their number has increased, and many of the poor are getting even poorer. The average income for poor families has slid to a little over $9,000 a year, 25 percent below the official boundary that defines poverty. About 23 million individuals—nearly one in ten Americans—now receive food stamps to help sustain themselves and their families. Like those of any large number of citizens, the conditions and personal qualities of the poor vary widely, except that nearly all must engage in a daily struggle to obtain the rudimentary necessities of an often precarious existence.

Most poignant among the poor are the children. Twenty-five percent of the nation's young—one out of every four children under the age of six—live in poverty. Many will not even live to experience the degradation of poverty. The American rate of infant mortality (defined as death by age one) is now twenty-fourth in the world, based on 1987 statistics, the most recent available. The infants of the poor are well represented in these appalling numbers, but the plague of infant death has begun to spread to the working middle class as well.

There is no concept of justice or virtue that justifies our willingness to allow or compel millions of our fellow citizens to suffer involuntary poverty. And what principle could we possibly invoke to absolve ourselves of the fate of children too young to comprehend their expulsion from an abundant land, unaware that the promise of America is not for them. They are denied the pleasures of childhood; their natural capacities are crippled, their spirits and minds are irrevocably stunted almost from birth. Their impoverishment is our disgrace, a betrayal of American principle, and a sin against God.

American principles impose a moral obligation to provide an opportunity for the poor to emerge from their distress. However, the extent and growth of poverty is not just a moral issue, but is further evidence of our economic decline. Poverty has also contributed to our economic woes by excluding millions of people from the market and from contributing to the process of production. Instead of adding to the nation's wealth, the poor simply increase the cost of maintaining the minimum attributes of a civilized society, which cannot allow its citizens to starve or freeze or be denied covering for their bodies. Thus, large-scale poverty diminishes the economic strength of the country and reduces the quality of life for all Americans.

The scars of our present dissolution are unusually vivid in the Northeast, where numerous small businesses—many of them established for years—have been forced into bankruptcy. Every bankrupt shop or restaurant, every losing business, conceals a story. It is not just a story of commerce. It chronicles the ebullient hopes of the beginning, the long hours of toil, the optimistic expectations gradually eroded by the painful onset of realization that the numbers were not balancing—and that they were never going to balance.

Of course the hardships of decline are not for everyone. Not for the wealthiest 20 percent, whose fortunes have risen during the last decade: a doubling of income, a tripling of wealth. Although they are still rich, some are not as rich as they were. And ultimately, of course, very few will escape the deepening deterioration. We are all on the same ship, and if it goes down, it will take most of the passengers with it. Neither personal wealth nor high income provides a permanent guarantee of invulnerability to a continued decline that has already inflicted distress on the great majority of Americans and has injured the sources of national greatness.

Accompanying and contributing to our economic descent is a continued rise in unemployment. Today almost 9 million are officially counted as unemployed, and the number is still rising. It is also misleading. It does not include the more than one million Americans who, unable to find work, have given up searching for jobs. It does not count the more than 6 million citizens who can find only part-time work, or those forced into lesser-paid occupations far below their abilities—the engineering consultant, for instance, who must now drive a cab to support his family. Thus the official employment statistics mask the reality that well over 16 million Americans—13 percent of our entire work force—is unemployed or underemployed. Further, members of over half the families who live below the poverty line are the working poor. They are employed. They go to work. But their wages are too low to raise them from the ranks of the officially impoverished. The damaging effects of rising unemployment extend far beyond those deprived of the opportunity to work. When a worker sees others laid off or hears of plant closings, his own sense of security is impaired; the consequent postponement of planned expenditures contributes to a decline in the worker's own standard of life and to national recession.

But our present distress cannot be measured solely in the statistics of economic growth or income. Like some incurable and readily transmitted plague, it has assaulted almost every element that composes the American standard of life. Fighting to sustain a deeply flawed economy, we seem unable to summon either the will or the resources to confront our most serious problems: poverty, inability to educate our children, destruction of the natural world, spreading violence, lack of care for the ill and disabled. The country that poured forth its treasure to rebuild Europe and Japan, that has spent unimaginable sums for fifty years to defend the freedom of half the globe—that same great America cannot restore devastated Detroit, or even find a doctor for the elderly lady who lives, immobilized, in obscenely ugly public housing on the edge of Cambridge, Massachusetts, within sight of Harvard University and its army of ambitious consultants to policymakers of business and government.

Declining growth in the gross national product and falling personal income are not the causes of our present distress. They are symptoms of other economic failures and systemic disorders that threaten us with continued, and perhaps permanent, decline in our ability to create wealth. The reckless, occasionally criminal policies of business and a corrupted political structure have contributed to the precipitous drop in our ability to create wealth. But shortsighted, predatory business and political corruption can be found in many earlier periods of American history. Nor is the present decline in our creation of wealth the result of some transformation in American values and character. Our businesses have not lost the desire to compete. But they have lost some of their ability to compete, a loss derived, in large part, from debilitating changes in the structure—the process of production—that governs some of our largest and most important industries. Our current deterioration is more serious and more ominous because its causes have become embedded in the form, the fundamental nature, of modern American capitalism.

Freud once wrote that anatomy is destiny, a contention now hotly disputed. But it is indisputable that in business, as in government and in many other aspects of human conduct, structure is function. And the changed structure of democratic capitalism has led to decline. The topic has

66

less powerful, the living standards of the people, the greatness of the nation.

Mergers and acquisitions, the glittering fashion of the 1980s, have merely accelerated a process of concentration that menaces capitalism and democracy alike, a process that has had the enthusiastic cooperation of a government that has failed to enforce existing laws or to enact new rules to protect us from harmful concentrations of economic power and guarantee a competitive marketplace. While size is not, by itself, the cause of decline (though the excessive concentration of economic power is always dangerous to democracy), the economic concentration of power of the last half-century—unlike the trusts of an earlier industrialism—has been increasingly accompanied by an evolution toward the forms and conduct of bureaucracy. The result has been damaging changes in the structure and conduct of business.

"Bureaucracy" is not merely a defamatory term for unloved institutions. It describes any enterprise, public or private, that functions in relative independence of any conflicting desires, special purposes, or insanities of those individuals who direct it. Indeed, we have enshrined the immobility of business bureaucracy in a now banal phrase—corporate culture—which, properly understood, tells us that the corporation has a life, a code of conduct, independent of its managers. And bureaucracy must be large—large enough to permit and justify internal regulation through "policies," "procedures," and "standards," which can diminish the creative vitality and flexibility necessary for competitive success. Function and size thrive in mutual dependency, an inorganic analogy to soul and body, mind and matter.

Although competition creates wealth for the nation, it is not embraced with compelling enthusiasm by any particular enterprise. If an enterprise becomes large and powerful enough to reduce competition, its conduct of business inevitably takes a different form, for its purpose has changed. Growth and preservation of the enterprise, not competitive victories, become its guiding objectives. The company expands. The company is respected. The company's executives are honored and well paid. But the enterprise itself, as a functioning component of democratic capitalism, has lost its competitive edge. And this loss diminishes a company's ability to create wealth. Why invest in new products or production processes when the old ones are doing just fine?

There is, however, a potential threat to this bureaucratic nirvana. Should conditions change and serious competitive challenges emerge, a large enterprise will find it extremely difficult, perhaps impossible, to adapt. It is huge, sprawling, complicated, and therefore quite ponderous and hard to change. More significantly, a large enterprise is not an artifact. It is a process—production, marketing, management, and much more—which has been staffed and guided by individuals whose achievement, training, and experience are based on ways of doing business that may now have become outmoded and even unprofitable, not only for the company, but for the country. Something like this happened to the swelling and virtually unchallenged industries of postwar America when they were unexpectedly confronted with unforeseen competitive challenges from the renascent economies of Japan and Europe. Their inability to respond, rooted in their bureaucratic transformation, ranks high among the agents of our present distress.

Economic bureaucracies pursue growth relatively unrestrained by those considerations of economic efficiency and profitability that the traditional market thought to enforce. The costs of operating the largest corporations—paperwork and computers, accountants and analysts—along with the loss of flexibility and enterprise imposed by size, far exceed the savings due to volume of production and transaction. Such bureaucracies are hugely inefficient. There are too many people, memos, buildings, machines, meetings. But the lavish excess of cost is trivial compared with the waste incurred through the mounting incapacities of control, which are masked by the modern technology of organization.

Managers with access to wires, cables, and the jetstream have abolished geography. Computers, cost accounting, and other new technologies of management have made it possible to assemble a swelling empire under a central directorate. The manager no longer knows his business or understands his workers from personal observation. He must depend on a stream of information from experts and subordinates. Personal direction is replaced by "standard procedures," ripening into a code of conduct that becomes the mores of the bureaucracy. It becomes necessary to judge performance by "objective measurements," and those measurements soon become ends in themselves, abstract criteria to which reality must conform (since reality always changes faster than rules).

It is not possible to maintain rigorous standards of efficiency and quality, clarity of control and responsibility, or internal discipline within the diffused members of such sprawling colossi. In the post-Nader age, auto companies did not want to produce a million defective cars that would have to be recalled and fixed. They just couldn't help themselves. It was the natural outcome of the established manufacturing process on which their business was based—which, indeed, was built into the nature of the enterprise. Since automobile executives were captives of their own bureaucracies, it was natural for them to claim during the 1960s and early 1970s that there "was no market in America for small cars." Of course not. Detroit didn't make small cars and dealers didn't stock them. There can be no "market" for a product no one can find. Then came Volkswagen, a great success, but only a pilot ship for the approaching Japanese man-of-war, proving that the demand was always there, dormant, awaiting discovery. But the titans of Detroit, like many American executives in other industrial bureaucracies, relying on their "market research," never discussed the subject with their customers. Certainly they had never driven a foreign car or thought it worthwhile to visit the factories of Japan. Too bad. There were some interesting things going on.

Self-preservation, the pursuit of expansion for its own sake regardless of cost, and the reduction of economic competition are the priorities of economic bureaucracy. These objectives are at odds with the creation of wealth by democratic capitalism. For it is the struggle for competitive advantage that compels those who control resources to seek out new demand, develop new products, and risk capital. It drives the search for increased efficiency and more advanced techniques of production. Without a competitive struggle there is no way for the market to enforce either the most efficient use of resources or the allotment of resources to the satisfaction of consumers' needs, or—more economically significant in a modern middle-class country—to the fulfillment of desire. Desire, and not necessity, is the quickening genius of an advanced economy. Matched to the possession of value, it becomes economic demand. By arresting this process, the economic bureaucracy immobilizes the resources of society: not only capital, but talent, invention, enterprise, risk, energy. Indeed, once the remorseless judgments of the market have been lifted, one can no longer even distinguish waste from productive use. The result is a loss of the spirit of enterprise. And a loss of enterprise leads to defeat in the marketplace.

Brooks Adams wrote that all great civilizations began to decline because of the steady, seemingly inexorable, centralization of economic power. "The process of centralization," Adams wrote, "led to the illusion of omnipotence, and thereby to arrogance, decadence, bureaucratic inefficiency, impotence and destruction by newer and more vigorous rivals or invaders." The decline of contemporary America is evidence of Adams's insight. The decrease in America's ability to create wealth has been most dramatically demonstrated by the competitive triumphs of newly industrialized nations—our "newer and more vigorous rivals or invaders." As recently as the mid-1970s, we sold more of our products to other nations than we bought from them. Then the flow began to reverse, not gradually but with the dimensions of a flood. In the 1980s, a single decade, we accumulated a total trade deficit of more than a trillion dollars, a deficit that was expected to rise another $90 billion in 1992. That deficit is more than a statistic. It tells us about the transfer of American wealth to foreign countries, from our own people to others. It is caused largely by the American consumer's preference for goods made in other countries, a judgment that we have failed to compete with the products of foreign industry. That competitive failure has lessened American wealth.

Combined with the need to finance our drastically unbalanced budget, the trade deficit has led to a precipitate fall in the value of the dollar. The cheapening dollar has not, as many economists prophesied, done much to reduce the trade deficit (although it has added to the cost of foreign goods purchased here). But it has persuaded many foreign investors to put their wealth in securities and money instruments that are backed by more stable currencies (60 percent of all Japanese portfolio investment now goes to Europe), thus reducing the supply of investment capital badly needed by American business. By any measure, more money is leaving America than is coming back. The once proud boast "sound as a dollar" has become a mockery.

We have paid tens of billions to protect other countries so they could safely take our money—a bargain at any price. We built bombs to guard them so they could make television sets for us. Of course, the choice was ours. We believed their security was essential to our own. It was probably so. But, as their prosperity mounted, we asked nothing in return, requested no compensation for guarding their security as well as our own. And we are supposed to be the nation of business!

Not satisfied with taking our money and our markets, foreign competitors are buying the very foundations of our abundance—American land, American companies, American banks—while moving gradually and deliberately toward the takeover of entire industries. The cheapening dollar has made it easier and more economic for foreign investors to buy American assets. And, to a significant extent, they are using their profits from products and loans sent to America. We are being bought with our own folly and money.

Foreign investment in our securities or in American-owned enterprise is no immediate threat to America's future growth. It may help create jobs and increase income, provide money for modernization, expansion, or essential working capital. And, obviously, if we are going to buy Japanese products, we are better off if they are made in America by American workers. Such investments, however, are very different from acquisitions—the transfer of American businesses to foreign owners. Democratic capitalism creates wealth by making products whose value in the market is greater than the costs of production. That process is the source of our nation's economic growth. When foreign businesses acquire our productive assets, the profits that are the privilege of ownership and the source of national economic growth return to other lands, enriching them with the fruits of our labor and the products of our invention. Wealth created in the United States and by Americans is diverted to the economic growth of other countries. American workers may keep their jobs, and American sellers may make a great deal of money, but the nation's possibilities are diminished, and the likelihood of further deterioration is increased.

This injury to American growth is made even more likely by the fact that a large proportion of these purchases come from our most vigorous competitive rivals. The Japanese are not the only buyers of America, not even the largest, but they are, by far, the most visible, the most formidable, and the most determined to extend their control over America's productive power. Recently a large Japanese company bought some of America's largest movie studios. The entertainment "industry" has been one of our largest and most successful exporters, and the substitution of Japanese ownership seems to have made little visible difference, at least for now. The studios continue to make films, and are still run by American workers under the direction of American managers (who are, naturally, the employees of absentee Japanese owners). But the wealth they create, including income from exporting their products, will belong to Japan. While those who formerly owned the studios greatly increased their wealth by selling, the sale diminished America, for its ability to increase abundance was impaired.

Not only does control of wealth influence economic progress, it is self-evidently a formidable source of power within society. Those who acquire the influence inherent in the control of wealth must inevitably use it to advance their own interests. Such use is inherent in the nature of power. It is hard enough to protect the well-being of our citizens against the depredations of the managers of our own capitalism. Can we possibly believe it will be any easier when wealth and economic power are in the hands of strangers? After all, the future greatness and prosperity of America are surely not among the highest priorities of foreign investors.

We may be living in a global economy, but there is no global society. We cannot expect the influence accumulated by foreign buyers to be exerted in support of American principles and traditions that they do not share. Thus, in selling large and productive assets, allowing foreign owners to control some of our most important industries, we are selling part of America itself.

Meanwhile, our leaders—in both politics and business—stand in silent witness, the silence broken by occasional applause, their show of enthusiasm stimulated by high-powered American lawyers and lobbyists who are lavishly paid to advance foreign interests in the media, among the people, and in the halls of Congress. We are being partially transformed into a technologically advanced labor colony for the benefit of others. Rarely have leaders so enthusiastically welcomed the encroachment of their conquerors.

Some of our foreign competitors have engaged in unfair trading practices to increase their access to our market and guard their own from American competitors. The Japanese, for example, have occasionally cut prices to unprofitable levels, allowing them to dump goods in order to increase their share of the American market. At the same time, they have restricted our access to their own markets by imposing a virtually incomprehensible web of restrictions, from formal rules to bureaucratic obstacles and delay. Undoubtedly such practices have strengthened their ability to compete. But we let them do it. And without a fight. Even now, when confronted with unfair trading practices, we prefer lengthy and often inconclusive negotiations to swift retribution, ignoring the reality that foreign competitors will be deterred from these practices only by the certain knowledge that compensatory damage will be inflicted. Since when did Americans become so naive, so weakened in will, as to believe that whining protest and obvious bluffs, rather than forceful action, could ensure fair treatment in a world of fiercely contending ambitions? Every school playground teaches us differently.

Still, we must not seek to evade our own responsibilities by indulging in a self-exculpatory quest for foreign villains. Our foreign competitors have succeeded chiefly because we were indifferent, arrogant, contemptuous, and largely unaware of our growing vulnerability. While it is important to deal with unfairness, it is far more important that we increase our own ability to compete.

Our postwar preeminence—we were the greatest, richest, most powerful nation on earth—was bound to be challenged by a recovering world. Yet as that inevitable challenge emerged, we clung to obsolete production techniques and carelessly fabricated products, while other countries modernized their factories, transformed emerging technology—often developed in American laboratories—into new consumer goods, and aggressively pursued customers in dozens of markets, including our own. Even as the success of others became evident, we still refused to study and adopt the many advances being made by foreign industry. As a consequence, countries that were once our dependents have become our competitors.

The majority of our foreign rivals, moreover, have merely sought to make money. Most of them operate within the law. Many have been helped to infiltrate the confines of our capitalist structure because we have deliberately widened the passageways in order to ease the flow of foreign money into the coffers of wealthy American individuals and corporations. It was not the actions of foreign competitors that prevented us from anticipating a demand for small cars, improving the quality of our products, installing modern techniques of production, or transforming technological innovations into consumer products. American science developed transistors and other semiconductors. But others had the technological and commercial skill to use them to manufacture goods that Americans wanted to buy.

Could we have matched our competitors? Of course. But we didn't. Instead, we lost our edge and allowed our will to become blunted. America's enormous capacities—developed, proven, and tempered over two centuries—were wasted. Others did not surpass us; we fell behind. Thus, our ability to create wealth for the nation has been gravely impaired; this self-inflicted injury has contributed to economic decline and a deteriorating standard of American life.

To reverse the damaging impact of our current crisis, it is imperative that we enhance our abilities to compete—effectively, ferociously, and with no quarter given—in every corner of the world. Doing so will require the restoration and strengthening of the entire structure of democratic capitalism. It is the only alternative to a continued descent, which will unravel the fabric of a free society.

Many of those who created large companies, or have directed their restoration, had a common quality: They were deeply, personally involved in their labors, often to the exclusion of other interests. Hardly an ideal prescription for the balanced life, but extraordinarily salutary for the business. Their energies, skills, and personal emotions were directed toward the creation or resurrection of enterprises that could thrive and expand whatever exigencies the future might bring. It was, after all, their business—or at least they felt that it was an extension of themselves. There are still such individuals among the leaders of American business. But their numbers are dwindling. The bureaucratization of economic institutions has transformed the interests and conduct of management, further damaging our capacity to create wealth.

Today, authority over the structure of bureaucratic enterprise is nearly always bestowed on transient managers. They don't own the company. They work for it. The legal owners—the shareholders—have, with a few exceptions, no power to direct the activities of their companies, and are therefore owners in name only. The company is theirs in the same way the government is ours, except that the shareholders' meeting is an even less effective instrument of control than the ballot box.

Managers are the wealthiest and most powerful of workers, and the most utterly dependent upon the existing structure of enterprise. Management skills, even at the highest levels, are not awesomely complex, technical, or difficult. Managerial talent is based less upon a personal capacity to create or command a segment of the wealth-producing apparatus than upon its suitability to the functional imperatives of established enterprise—in other words, the ability to protect and conduct the existing process. And the other face of managerial skill, the capacity to rise within the bureaucracy, acquires its value, even its definition, from the organization itself.

Like other workers, managers exchange their skills for income. Unlike most other workers, they also exchange those skills for a limited power within the company. That power enables them to claim compensation unrelated to skills or productivity. There are limits, of course, since even the highest manager of the largest corporation is neither king nor owner, but chairman of a collective leadership. Precedents and scales must be considered; and damage to the corporation itself—by depleting capital or provoking unnecessary public controversy—must be avoided. Within those limits, however, an executive can become very rich. Even the president of a failing company can command a large increase in pay. After all, it's not his money. Nor does it belong to the directors who vote the increase. It will be the workers and perhaps the customers who must pay in the end. And they often don't even know it's happening.

In a recent magazine interview, an "executive recruiter" advises those hoping for recruitment: "If you're in Procter & Gamble and each of the four group managers had brand experience in Duz and none with Jif peanut butter, consider it a hint. That doesn't mean you can't make it from Jif, but it will enlarge your chances if you can get Duz brand experience." The point is not satirical. No one who has spent time in government and politics should ridicule the paths of ambition taken by others. But such knowledge, and the ability to act upon it, does not add either to productivity or to the creation of wealth. It is valuable only because a bureaucratic structure rewards it. In its imaginative vitality, the skill of climbing executive heights (as distinct from managerial ability) is often impressive. Yet it is a regressive skill, turned toward mastery of the corporate structure rather than toward enlarging or maximizing the economic contribution and renewal of the productive apparatus. There is some relationship, of course. Performance is a criterion for promotion. But as general economic competition dwindles and responsibility within corporations becomes more diffuse, the difficulty of judging performance by external standards such as profits and earnings makes internal standards even more important.

Like most ambitious people, the managers of bureaucratic industries are driven by the pursuit of self-interest, the animating spirit of capitalist free enterprise. Because most of them are employees with uncertain tenure, they are compelled to direct their attention and energy toward the short-term earnings of their companies, thus hoping to increase the size of their personal compensation and retain the favor of directors and major shareholders. They strive to accumulate money before control passes—as it inevitably must—to other hands. They have little more concern for the long-term growth and prosperity of their companies than a bank robber has for the soundness of the bank. (Although, unlike the robber, they would deny their indifference.) The importance of their achievements to the well-being of the country as a whole rarely enters into their decisions; such thoughts are largely reserved for country-club conversations, where they join their wealthy colleagues in lamenting the worsening condition of America—especially as it affects their particular business—and the lack of "vision," "new ideas," and capacity for decisive leadership among candidates for high office—the very defects that have allowed them to become prosperous in their own occupations.

We may, with some justification, call this greed. But we must also recognize that greed is one of the most powerful motive forces of capitalism. By enriching himself, the theory goes, the entrepreneur adds to the abundance of society. And so long as public institutions keep careful scrutiny and ensure that the energies of private accumulation also flow to the public good, this theory can work. But when the channels of competition are clogged, when the market is distorted or crippled, when the economy reserves some of its richest rewards for ingenious but nonproductive financial manipulation, when bureaucratic organization obstructs innovation and risk, then greed becomes a destructive force—accumulating wealth for a few at large expense to those who do the work, and to the detriment of the nation's health and growth.

Although some individuals may deserve severe repri-
mands, it would be both wrong and misleading to excoriate
the managers of enterprise as a class. Their inadequacies
accurately reflect the structure of the businesses they guide.
Their concern is, as it must be, that things go relatively well
during their stewardship, for their tenure and income depend on it. If mistakes are made, it is imperative that they
escape blame. The necessary psychic consequence is that the
fear of failure outweighs the desire for success. And since
risk, innovation, and change are always accompanied by the
possibility of failure, they are to be avoided except when one
is compelled by the most dire necessity. Because total avoid-
ance of change is impossible, managers surround themselves
with a host of participants in decision—vice presidents,
division chiefs, market researchers (remember New
Coke?)—who are allowed just enough authority to help
spread the responsibility if things go wrong. In the end, of
course, as a last resort one can always fire the advertising
agency.

Not long ago a newspaper carried a story about the retiring president of one of America's largest corporations, for
years the dominant figure in his industry. Still healthy and
vigorous, he was asked if he truly wanted to retire. "I am,"
he replied, "fully in agreement with the company's retire-
ment policies." And how could it be otherwise? Over
decades his will had fused with that of the organization in
whose service he had been granted the highest success. That
organization, like any large economic unit, is not just a
collection of factories, equipment, and money. It is a process
of production, a material field of transactions and economic
relationships. The rules, customs, and directions that prescribe functions—that seem only to define and limit the
process—are, in fact, the process itself, just as rules that

govern the rights and conduct of courts, lawyers, and parties are the legal process.

The manager whose control over wealth, whose claim to value and position, is established by the institution cannot defy it in any fundamental way. After all, he achieved his rank and power by mastering its process. Successful participation precludes any challenge to basic values, structure, or direction. Effectiveness itself is defined as the capacity to guide, perhaps improve, the established process. Individual will is exercised along these lines of structure or it is annulled by the process. The manager is inwardly compelled to continue that process and extend its reach, not reluctantly, but from the powerful convictions that have supplanted his potential for autonomous defiance. And should, somehow, that autonomy survive, even the most revered manager (unless he was also an owner) would not have the power to make fundamental shifts. He must remember that the company is not his. He is, after all, only a manager, an employee, and if his conduct seemed to threaten the organization, the others of his class, as directors or executives, would displace him. So does fear triumph over achievement, and timidity drown out risk.

Thus, from choice or from necessity—it makes little difference to the threatened American dream—the managerial class has abandoned its responsibility to revitalize old industries, to make the changes necessary to increase efficiency and expand their markets. American managers have been slow to develop the technologies of the future and even slower in translating technological change into profitable products. The result is a diminished ability to compete and to increase the creation of wealth—the source of growth for company and country alike.

Some of the responsibility for this failure can be attributed to individual incompetence or beliefs. But most derives from a bureaucratic structure that is not only inefficient, but contains an almost irresistible urge toward stagnation and a pervasive fear of innovation. Bureaucracy, and thus its managers—for they cannot be separated, having become fused in purpose—uses its resources to protect established methods and hierarchies; it is unwilling to sacrifice present profits for the uncertain prospect of future gains. And since the world of commerce is always changing, in this way the future is lost.

Of course, managers of declining companies are rarely the real losers. For the most part they depart even failing enterprises with a shower of gold to compensate for any slight injury to pride. The principal losers are working Americans whose jobs are threatened and whose income continues to decline.

America's ability to create wealth began to decline during the 1970s, gradually accelerating as we unsuspectingly traversed the fanciful 1980s on our passage toward today's near depression. However, for more than a decade, the extent of our steadily deepening fragilities was masked by the unprecedented, virtually unimaginable sums of borrowed money poured into the economy by a recklessly prodigal government, which created an illusion of prosperity while seriously damaging the entire financial structure on which the restoration of economic growth depends.

Virtually every deficiency of American capitalism requires increased capital investment—for expansion, modernization, the rebuilding of old industries, the establishment of new industries. Yet as need expands, access to capital has been diminished. An irresponsibly extravagant government and the intemperate speculations of private finance have dangerously reduced the investment capital available for the necessary modernization and expansion of business. Since the economic well-being of all Americans depends on increasing the creation of wealth by the private economy, our public prodigality and private greed have not only rewarded the privileged; they have impaired the nation's capacity to make investment essential to recovery and future progress.

Our history records many fierce debates over the wisdom of deficit financing. But we could not even imagine the glorious possibilities of borrowing until the really big spenders came to Washington only a few years ago, where they remain, still borrowing and still spending. It was like gold-leafing the interior of a mansion while the sills were rotting and the foundation was beginning to crumble. It all looked so wonderfully bright, positively iridescent, and welcoming—from the outside. And when the doors were flung open, the party was tumultuous with gaiety; it promised to go on forever—at least for those who were invited, those few able to afford a new outfit, a car and driver.

But the hosts for the occasion—being good, egalitarian Americans—reassured the multitudes outside that they too, if they worked hard and became successful, could someday stand on the polished mahogany and gaze out at those who hadn't made it. Wasn't that what America was all about? If you paid your taxes and stuck to your job—and if the government gave you a free pass to the Treasury—no opportunity would be foreclosed.

Although Ronald Reagan was a willing helmsman, the unanticipated lift-off of the national debt toward unprecedented orbits was not a partisan effort. "It's a go," said the President. "A–OK," responded the Congress. And we were on our way. The President presented budgets. The Congress debated, amended, and passed them. With some individual exceptions, and with disagreement on many particulars, a Republican administration joined with a Democratic Congress to create the largest deficits in American history.

How much did we borrow against the future? In the last dozen years we have added about $2.5 trillion to the public debt. That is almost triple the entire debt accumulated by the federal government from the time Washington bought the first punch bowl for his inaugural until the day Reagan moved into the White House—through a civil war, two world wars, financial panics, and a major depression. In a mere decade, the America that stood as the world's largest creditor performed an amazing, gravity-defying acrobatic sequence that left it the world's largest debtor. And during 1992 the public debt, which was slightly above $900 billion in 1980, will rise another $400 billion, reaching a total of around $4.5 trillion before the next presidential inauguration.

We have behaved as if the huge sums of money our government spends were not constrained by the strength of our economy or by any calculation of their possible contribution to the stimulation of growth. We just spent. And should these perennial budget deficits continue—and there is no convincing evidence of future reduction—it is quite possible that publicly held Treasury paper, the obligations issued to those who loan money to the government, could climb to nearly 100 percent of the entire gross national product by the end of the century, a level last reached during the Second World War.

This mindlessly mounting debt has helped lead us into recession and has deprived us of the resources necessary to heal grievous injuries to American society. Even more damaging, the debt concealed the extent of decline, thereby discrediting any analysis that purported to discover dangerous fissures in the very foundation of our economic process.

As a result, suggestions for urgent remedies were completely omitted from the public dialogue.

How can one explain a government going into serious debt every year, when the President, the Congress, the political parties, and the law of the land all demand we move toward a balanced budget? Maybe it's just a law of nature, like gravity, only in reverse. Or maybe it's a government that no longer works. A political structure suborned and corrupted by powerful private interests, as ours has been, cannot devise and enforce a national agenda that requires difficult, and often painful, choices. And we have evaded such choices. Incredibly, we both lowered taxes and increased spending, with little thought for the consequences.

However, there is no escape. There is only evasion. For the failure to choose is itself a decision. It is an election—unspoken and unacknowledged—to satisfy today's demands at the expense of our future possibilities, to permit the deterioration in the standard of American life to continue. And, far too often, it is also a judgment to benefit the wealthy and powerful to the detriment of the common welfare and the greatness of the nation.

An accumulation of debt on this scale over so long a period of time does not jump-start the economy. Rather, it drains the battery, damages the alternator, wrecks the generator, and short-circuits the voltage regulator. In less automotive terms—although there could be no more appropriate metaphor for our decline—the reckless spending of recent years has seriously injured our prospects for a resumption of growth. This is confirmed by recent experience. For years, huge budget deficits have been accompanied by economic decline. During the 1980s, our deficits were staggering, often more than $200 billion a year, and they have become even larger since George Bush ascended to the presidency. Yet the economy grew more slowly than during the previous two decades. In contrast, during our greatest periods of postwar growth, federal deficits were small—virtually nonexistent by today's standards. For example, we grew faster during the 1960s than in the two decades that followed, yet only $86 billion was added to the national debt—an average of less than $9 billion a year.

Since the earliest days of our Republic, government expenditures have contributed to the national well-being. Some money has gone to help the private economy create jobs and add to production. But government is not a business. It may accomplish marvels—feed the starving, support the machinery of justice, drive the fierce Iraqis from their desert fortresses. But when it drains vast sums of money from the private economy, it deprives industry of capital essential for investment in the urgently needed modernization and expansion of American capitalism.

Yet we simply continue to spend beyond our means—not to increase our power to produce, not to restore economic growth, but to continue the flow of money to those private interests whose wealth depends on government money, while placating those who oppose tax raises. And though these same staggering deficits continue, growth is virtually gone, the economy recedes, middle-class income declines, and the ranks of poverty increase.

Once the center of global finance, whose banks and currency were the leading motive force for economic development in virtually every nation outside the now vanishing communist world, America is no longer able to finance its own enterprise. Much of our financial leadership has passed to other countries. Although this descent is not due solely to a recklessly prodigal government and its insatiable demand for money, there is no doubt that America's indifference to fundamental principles of sound economic policy and its flagrant disregard of limits infected the policies and distorted the conduct of our entire private financial structure.

At the very foundation of our capital structure, some of the large "money center" banks, which bind and support the entire banking system, abandoned conservative banking principles. They financed mergers and acquisitions with debt instruments whose value should have been suspect. They hastened to make large and unrepayable loans to impoverished foreign countries. They agreed to wildly excessive investments in real estate, unrestrained by the actual economic value of the property or the risk of decline.

Then the bubble burst.

One can now better appreciate the wisdom of Jefferson's admonition that "I sincerely believe that banking establishments are more dangerous than standing armies." About two centuries later, unconsciously echoing his renowned predecessor, Lyndon Johnson remarked that "if this country ever collapses it will be the banks that bring it down. I didn't believe it when I heard it from my daddy, but after thirty years of experience I know he was right."

Some banks failed. Several of our financial institutions suffered severe losses and are now struggling for survival. Some of the largest would be on the edge of bankruptcy were they not sustained by a government that rightly regards such an economic disaster as unthinkable. And almost every day brings word of a new deterioration in the financial world. Another bank has failed. The Bank of Credit and Commerce International is in collapse. The scandalous collapse of the savings-and-loan industry deprived us of substantial capital resources. Even Salomon Brothers, a once honored symbol of financial integrity, has illegally impaired the vital market for Treasury securities—our securities, obligations of the taxpayer. The consequence to the national economy was a loss of some productive companies, an enormous waste of potential investment capital, and a serious impairment of the entire financial structure.

Access to capital is the fuel of economic growth, national abundance, and personal prosperity. Yet the necessary capital has become hard to find. Not only have enormous sums been dissipated, but even those who command large resources have become intensely conservative out of necessity intensified by fear—a consequence of their past recklessness and the increased rigors of official regulators seeking absolution for their derelictions during the years of unleashed speculation. Thus, many who wish to modernize or expand productive businesses, or to begin new enterprises, find it difficult—sometimes impossible—to obtain needed capital, even if their record of achievement, high credit rating, undoubted personal integrity, and the economic soundness of their proposals satisfy the most conservative banking principles.

The defects and infirmities in our financial structure, which we have created, constitute one of those basic flaws in the structure of capitalism that must be corrected if America is to be restored. If American business continues to be plagued by the capital shortages that have resulted from our own failures, arrogance, criminal greed, and astonishing incompetence, then the American standard of living will inevitably continue to decay.

Much more important than the amount we spent is what we failed to spend it on. We didn't spend it to modernize our factories or to develop the products of sophisticated technology, such as video-game equipment and camcorders, which are the objects of rising consumer demand. We didn't use it to train our young people for work in an economy that rewards skill and intelligence instead of muscle. Nor did we spend it to prevent our inner cities from becoming war zones, or to sustain the bonds of long-established communities against the rupturing assault of youth gangs, or to diminish the painfully urgent demand for drugs as the only means of escape from a world that offers none. Nor did we devote a significant fraction of those vast sums to reconcile technology with the natural world it is devastating. But these objectives also are essential to arresting the deterioration of American life.

Certainly, large amounts of the money borrowed from the private economy were wasted. To some extent waste is built into the nature of government, for government has no competition and the drive for competitive success is the only effective deterrent to the wasteful use of resources. However, waste is not the principal cause of our outrageous debt or its damaging consequences. Our profligacy reflects a disintegration of the values that have sustained and built America. To an unprecedented extent, we have ignored the demands of future growth in order to gratify present desires, and rejected the welfare of the American community in favor of personal and family gain.

Values are not merely a reflection of noble and abstract principles. They are a practical necessity. They sustain not only the idea of America, but the material welfare of its people. History has irrevocably fused the American promise with the American reality. They can no longer be severed. If the promise is betrayed, the realities will decay. Indeed, this has already begun to happen. How swiftly material distress has followed upon departure from our defining values.

Thus, the true deficit is not merely the trillions of dollars. It is a deficit of judgment, of thought, of fairness, of concern for those deprived of opportunity or even the most rudimentary needs of existence—a deficit of planning, of foresight, of building for the future, of preparing for a more competitive world. While we built "smart" bombs, we failed to install smart government.

And now where is the great prosperity of the 1980s? It is buried in bonds, concealed in Treasury notes, secreted in bank vaults, reposing in the hands of our creditors in every corner of the world. And the weakness that apparent prosperity concealed, the rotting at the core, is now beginning to manifest itself in every aspect of American life.

Fundamental to the strength and principles of democratic capitalism is that all should have an opportunity to contribute to the nation and be fairly rewarded for their efforts. Every citizen should share both the benefits of rising prosperity and the burden of difficult times. This is the defining premise of economic justice. "Justice," Madison wrote, "is the end of government. It is the end of civil society."

Differences of income and wealth are inherent in the nature of capitalism. They help drive the machine from which we all benefit. If individuals increase their wealth by contributing to the growth and capacity of America, then their rising fortunes are unobjectionable. When Henry Ford established the automobile industry, or when Thomas Edison taught us how to illuminate America, what was it worth to the country? The question is unanswerable. But their own rewards were certainly deserved.

But the Fords and the Edisons are rare. Although some of today's rich have established new sources of national wealth, they number only a handful. Some others have increased the productivity of an enterprise, creating increased wealth for the nation. But these are only a small minority of the fortunate rich. More typical is the retiring chairman of General Motors, who recently received a multimillion-dollar bonus for having presided over the rapid deterioration of a company whose past achievements made a significant contribution to American economic strength. As late as the 1960s, the automobile industry, along with its suppliers and dealers, was responsible for about one fifth of the entire gross national product.

It is impossible to define a "just" distribution of income with any precision. One cannot measure the income economically appropriate to a large variety of occupations. These values can and should be established by the market or by the decisions of democratic institutions. However, justice is like love. We cannot measure it, but we can usually recognize it when we feel it. And when our governing institutions embrace policies that deliberately transfer income and wealth from the many to the few, we know that principles of economic justice are being violated. Over the last two decades, just such a violation has occurred.

During the quarter-century of growth following the Second World War, most Americans enjoyed a steadily rising standard of living. Naturally, some made more than others, but most were moving upward. And so was America. We called ourselves an affluent society, and we believed that any remaining pockets of distress and poverty would soon be eliminated by continued growth accompanied by wise and compassionate policies.

However, over the last two decades and especially during the 1980s, as economic growth began to slow, something went wrong. Although middle-class income stagnated or declined, that of the richest fifth of the population went up about 15 percent. The average family income of the top 1 percent—about 600,000 families—more than doubled, while, at the bottom of the scale, the income of poor families slid 5 percent to an average of less than $10,000 a year. This income gap was accompanied by a growing disparity in wealth. The net worth of the average American family actually declined, while that of the fortunate fifth rose about 14 percent. And those in the top 1 percent doubled their holdings and attained some form of control over an astonishing 90 percent of the country's wealth.

Certainly this grotesque disparity, the virtual creation of a privileged economic oligarchy, has not occurred because most Americans are working less or because the rich are making an increased contribution to the nation's well-being. Nor is it some unforeseen twist of economic fate. Rather, it is the consequence of deliberate actions by and policies of both government and business. The principles of democratic capitalism have been perverted to give advantage not only to those who provide the most jobs or add to the nation's wealth, but also to those who can manipulate the governing structure of wealth and politics to enrich themselves at the expense of the people.

Economic injustice has helped transform growth into recession, and its continuance will help to bring about further decline. Our economic health rests on the existence of a large market for consumption. If middle-class income is threatened, or even diminished, the demand for consumer goods goes down; that decline is followed, quite logically, by a drop in production. Moreover, workers who sense they are being treated unfairly—by their employer or their government—lose some of their personal concern and intensity. The work ethic does not thrive under the rule of injustice.

During the seeming prosperity of the 1980s, observing the flow of wealth from the majority of Americans to a small privileged group, Ravi Batra, a brilliant economic philosopher, predicted that the 1990s would bring a severe economic slump, even a full-fledged depression. He based his analysis largely on the increasing maldistribution of income. He reminded us that a similar maldistribution, an abandonment of economic justice, had occurred in the period preceding the

Great Depression and was a principal cause of that disaster, just as the rising fortunes of the middle class during and after the Second World War led to steadily rising abundance. (In 1929, according to John Kenneth Galbraith, about 5 percent of the population received about one third of all personal income.) The comparison is persuasive. And whatever lessons we choose to draw from the past, the evidence of the present is undeniable. Our failure to enforce economic justice has contributed to the continuing deterioration of the nation.

Today's outrageous discrepancy between the fortunes of the middle class and those of the wealthy has not been mandated by the principles of our capitalist economy. Rather, many of today's wealthy have combined with the politicians they supported to win themselves exemption from decline, to augment their wealth and income even as the national economy falters and most Americans are forced to confront increasing economic distress.

The laws and institutions of the democratic process play a significant role in determining the distribution of income. Over the years we have devised an enormous network of laws and regulations intended to protect shareholders, taxpayers, consumers, and the national interest against the unrestrained greed of those who control the sources of wealth. In the last several years, political leadership, government bureaucracy, and businessmen have cooperated to rewrite or ignore such rules. Those public employees responsible for enforcement of government obligation, acting on their own or under pressure from elected officials, ignored, even approved, the most flagrant transgressions of the standards established to ensure economic justice. (Naturally the beneficiaries were the wealthy.)

This was not a partisan undertaking. Republicans collaborated with Democrats to enact laws that made it easier to transfer wealth to the rich, while increasing the burden on the working middle class. Together they abdicated or violated their constitutional responsibility to ensure strict and equitable enforcement of law by regulatory agencies. Flouting their sworn obligations, they refused to protect the competitive marketplace against financial manipulation. Although the forms of manipulation were novel, the purpose and effect were the same as those which had evoked the protective action of democracy for more than a century: the manipulation, distortion, and weakening of the competitive marketplace essential to American growth in order to benefit a privileged few. Despite opposition from a dwindling band of adherents to traditional principles, both parties embraced a kind of trickle-up economics, transferring wealth from the bottom to the top—a government of Robin Hoods in reverse.

The most obvious way to help your friends or financial supporters is to change the tax laws. "The apportionment of taxes on the various descriptions of property," Madison wrote, "is an act which seems to require the most exact impartiality; yet there is, perhaps, no legislative act in which greater opportunity and temptation are given to a predominant party to trample on the rules of justice." Both a Republican President and a Democratic Congress took full advantage of this opportunity "to trample on the rules of justice." During the 1980s, tax rates on the wealthy were reduced, despite a rapidly mounting deficit. But 60 percent of all Americans pay substantially more in taxes today than they did in 1980. The result: While taxes on the middle class rose, the wealthiest 1 percent, the most affluent of all Americans, pay 9 percent less today than they did ten years ago.

The changes that resulted in lowering taxes on the rich while increasing those paid by the middle class were accomplished through laws written by Democrats, enacted by a Democratic Congress, and signed by a Republican President. They served as a convincing demonstration that liberal Democrats could also help the rich and were equally grateful for their election-time generosity.

The tax laws are only the most obvious way of distributing wealth upward. Lax enforcement of banking laws allowed financiers to accumulate large fortunes. The taxpayer watched helplessly, or without comprehension, often unaware that he or she might be legally obligated to pay for the inevitable collapse of lucrative speculation. Newly anointed financial "wizards" were enriched by deals involving the merger and sale of businesses, leveraged buyouts of public companies, and worldwide transfers of illegal funds. Sometimes when one company buys another the ability of the combined firm to compete is increased. Most of these deals, however, simply involved a transfer or redistribution of ownership. No value was added to the American economy; no more wealth was created for the nation. When the deals were complete, the same companies were still there making the same products, and usually no more competitively than before. Indeed, the result of many mergers and acquisitions was to create incompatible economic hybrids that reduced the combined profitability and economic strength of once separate businesses. But they did attain one objective, which was usually the driving purpose of these transactions: They made some people very wealthy. Those who made the deals—having done little more than trade paper for paper—were paid fortunes as fees, direct compensation, and, one can be sure, in other ways that have still to come to light.

The huge amounts of money needed to buy control of businesses from owners and shareholders were borrowed from banks, savings-and-loan institutions, pension funds, wealthy investors, and even, poignantly, the contemporary counterpart of "widows and orphans"—retired people seeking a safe but rewarding haven for their small life savings. Many of these loans were secured by so-called high-yield bonds, which offered very high interest rates but no guarantee that the company would be able to pay that interest or repay the principal when the bond came due. Although called bonds—a term that connotes relative security—they were, for the most part, simply speculative wagers on the continued growth and profitability of the company that issued them. And because in many cases the premise was wrong, a large number of these bonds are now virtually worthless; they justify their vivid label: junk bonds (a term that is also somewhat unfairly applied to those high-yield bonds that have retained their value).

However, those who made the deals—and there were thousands—didn't suffer. They made a great deal of money. Indeed, many who had acquired power over now failing enterprises retained the wealth they had derived from control, their private fortunes insulated by law from the debts of the corporation. The rich got richer, or, if they weren't rich to start with, they were when the deal was over—even the few who went to jail. And the deal-makers have no legal obligation to those who lost their jobs, to the nation's damaged businesses, or to the retired couple on the patio of their Florida home, which has just been foreclosed. Nor are they responsible for compensating the country whose resources they have stolen or destroyed.

The years of recklessly high-powered trading were accompanied by an abundance of warnings that companies and financial institutions were being placed in great danger by an orgy of speculation not unlike that which preceded the Great Depression. But the official guardians of democracy did not heed the warnings. On the contrary, Congress and the White House passed laws and pressured regulators to help the deal-makers, many of whom were prominent on lists of political contributors. Then, even as the dike was beginning to leak, the representatives of democratic power were often too busy drilling new openings to engage in any serious discussion of flood control.

Thus, large amounts of capital—money that might have gone to modernize or expand productive enterprise—were diverted to enable one managing or directing group to displace another, or to replace equity with debt so that control could be transferred from shareholders to individual businessmen. Moreover, the ability of companies to pay the interest on the money they borrowed—to service their debt—depended on growing profits. Loans that offered a high yield to creditors also imposed a high cost on borrowers. In keeping with the speculative spirit of the time, the deal-makers were confident that growth and mounting earnings were inevitable. But they were wrong. Their confidence was merely the imagining of desire. As the economy slowed toward stagnation, and earnings failed to grow as predicted, many businesses found that profits were no longer adequate to meet their interest payments. Some discovered that their assets were now worth less than their debts. The result was a series of bankruptcies, restructurings, cutbacks, and downsizings. Those who had made the loans lost their money. Entire financial institutions were damaged, some of them forced to struggle, not always successfully, to maintain their solvency. Many workers lost their jobs, while others were forced to accept lower wages and reduced benefits. And for America the result was a loss of national productive power.

Yet, astonishingly, it seems that with a few exceptions those who benefited from even the most flagrant violations of economic justice are perfectly secure to enjoy their gains. The government never did and never will conduct an intensive inquiry into the multitudinous violations of securities laws, tax laws, and fraud laws that almost certainly occurred. And with good reason. For it was government laws and government regulations—or the lack of regulations—that made it possible for a few to accumulate increasing wealth while most Americans found themselves victims of stagnation and decline.

In response to mounting public indignation surrounding the savings-and-loan scandal, Congress did hold a few perfunctory hearings. Federal officers did pursue a few of the more notorious knaves, tried them, and even got some convictions. It would be wrong to think of the men who were tried as scapegoats. They were fairly accused and fairly tried. But I would wager that at times, alone in their cells, those who went to court reflected on how many loyal friends suddenly materialized while they awaited trial; and they detected, perhaps, some slight hint of anxiety among those past colleagues who came to offer sympathy, support, and expressions of indignation at the unfairness of it all. After all, were it a criminal offense to augment one's wealth by impairing the economic health of the entire country, the jails would be flooded with arrivals from the world of finance.

There were, of course, many other ways in which wealth was transferred upward. Many were perfectly legal. Others were in direct violation of the law and the established standard of official regulation. For example, those assigned to monitor compliance with sound banking practices did not interfere with the virtual orgy of real estate speculation, which made fortunes for some, but ultimately seriously impaired our financial structure, making it far more difficult for businesses to obtain money needed for investment, or even to sustain successful enterprises during temporary difficulties.

Some of our large and long-established financial institutions deliberately manipulated the market in Treasury securities essential to the operation of government and the health of the economy. (That market raised $1.7 trillion in 1991 alone.) They did so to increase their earnings above the amount that a freely competitive marketplace would yield. Yet any disruption of this market, even a barely perceptible doubt of its integrity, impairs the economy, costs taxpayers hundreds of millions of dollars, and thus reduces economic opportunity.

Moreover, the government itself controls assets of immense size. It spends about a fifth of the entire gross national product, and its decisions can bring fortunes to some, bankruptcy to others. The bulk of this federal spending goes to increase the profits of our largest companies, with little supervision of the costs that enter into the calculation of price. The result is not simply waste, but the enrichment of the privileged beneficiaries by the taxpayer. One need only recall the $1,000 hammers, or the lawless awards of contracts for public housing, to understand the many conduits through which wealth taken from taxpayers or borrowed to finance the deficit can flow to further enhance the fortunes of the already wealthy. Nor does this near-larcenous behavior include the subsidies—grants or loan guarantees—that support domestic businesses that have political power or give political money. (Americans still pay as much as $75 billion extra a year for a variety of goods, thanks solely to import fees and restrictions. The criteria for imposing these costs rarely include concern for enhancing the competitiveness of the protected American businesses; more often, the rules are enacted to reduce the need to compete.)

All of these decisions are subject to the oversight of elected government. Naturally, they rarely receive it—except from individual legislators whose principal interest is to ensure that benefits flow to their constituents and supporters. The just distribution of wealth and income is not often a consideration.

One could multiply illustrations to further demonstrate how the rich advanced their fortunes while most Americans were the victims of stagnation or decline. But it is unnecessary. Our departure from economic justice is undeniable, proven by those facts that document the present reality of mounting distress for the many and increasing abundance for the few.

Even more disturbing than past transgressions is government's present failure to insist on action to restore economic justice through the strict enforcement of existing rules and the enactment of new ones. Some abuses of recent years may have been newly contrived, but they violated and damaged the established economic cornerstone of democratic capitalism: the free, competitive marketplace, whose protection has been among the highest responsibilities of our government since it was established in 1787. And no observant official of democracy could have failed to understand this. With rare exceptions, the transgressions of the last two decades have not been secret. They have been known to informed individuals—both public and private—discussed from public platforms, described in magazines and newspapers. Yet the chosen guardians of democracy demonstrated little desire to restrain the wealthy who had supported them in the past, and whose future support seemed essential to their ambition for office. Ours has proven, with some exceptions, a government far more zealous in the service of the few than in the fulfillment of its mandated obligations to the many.

The consequences of this combination of private power with its political allies have injured the country. The relative decline of the middle class has diminished its ability to consume, thus constructing the mass market on which the success of democratic capitalism depends. Large sums of money were diverted from capital investment to help enrich a privileged few. And the injury caused to businesses by excessive debt reduced the productive power of the country. The result was predictable, and it was predicted: The maldistribution of wealth and income has contributed to economic decline and human distress.

IV

The Challenge of Restoration

TODAY, ECONOMIC OPPORTUNITY is being diminished for many and denied to some. The American standard of living—an imprecise concept, but one that we all intuitively understand—is steadily deteriorating as personal income and national wealth decline. That reality provides both the necessity and the goal of change. For it constitutes a denial of the promise of America.

We cannot assume that a renewed expansion of opportunity is inevitable. Some believe a nation's destiny contains an inevitable rhythm of recurrence, that every decline contains the seeds of resurgence, and every time of increase conceals the seeds of constriction. America's chronicle contains a great deal of evidence to support such a belief. But, as nations go, ours has a very short history. A longer and more expansive view teaches a different lesson—from the self-destructive actions that forever ended the ancient Athenian imperium, to the irreversible loss of British preeminence during living memory. There are a multitude of once prospering and ascendant states that never recovered from decline. What goes up must come down. But there is no parallel imperative commanding that which falls to rise again.

Even within our own relatively brief experience, a renewal of progress or escape from danger has occurred, not as the result of some immutable process, but through sometimes painful, often drastic actions by those dedicated to preserving and strengthening the Republic. Twenty years ago, it would have been far easier to arrest and reverse the deterioration of American life. But we have done ourselves a great deal of damage in the last two decades, making the task of restoration far more difficult.

Yet even though restoration is not inevitable, it is well within our powers. Descent is not yet irreversible. We possess enormous resources, the greatest of which is a people who have shown themselves capable of meeting great challenges. I refuse to believe that the same people who, only a few short years ago, were preeminent among the nations of the world have suddenly become enfeebled, incapable of their own restoration. Walk down any street in America, listen to the conversation in the local coffee shop or bar, and you will not hear the sounds of defeat, but anger, frustration, a vehemently expressed desire to resurrect the American promise in all its fullness. But neither frustration nor desire is enough, although both are necessary. Our problems will not solve themselves. No pillar of fire illuminates the way, nor have all the intricate marvels of modern science provided us with a staff capable of parting the seas. The destiny of democracy is in our hands. And if we are to retain control over that destiny, immediate measures are required.

Earlier in this essay I examined the failures of the political process along with proposals for remedy. In the following pages, I offer suggestions for specific economic policies, which are intended only to demonstrate that practical approaches to these urgent problems do exist. They are meant as starting points for a debate that will lead toward their refinement and expansion. However, even though these ideas vary widely in content and direction, they do share an important premise: that, on the whole, people will pursue their self-interest—at least if they know what it is, an understanding that is rarer than one would expect, but can be enhanced by demonstrating the truth that furthering the interests of the individual often depends on enhancing the interests of others. By redirecting or, when necessary, restraining self-interest so that it is compelled to change the form of its expression, we can redirect democratic capitalism so that it continues to advance the well-being of the American people. That is the basic principle of political action—to make personal interest and desire, even greed, act as a servant of the commonwealth.

Before examining an agenda for change, let us first indulge in a brief excursion to a land of myth and folly so seductive that it obstructs the path of necessary action. Any serious effort to modify the economic structure will inevitably provoke outrage from the beneficiaries and tribunes of the established structure. None are more vocal, more stridently insistent, more categorically dogmatic about the evils of big spending and the horrors of government "interference" in private business than the "conservative" leaders—public and private, Republican and Democrat—who now dominate, confuse, and, deliberately or from ignorance and belief, misguide the opinions of the people.

For more than a decade, fearlessly confident of presidential support, our congressional representatives have walked boldly past the monument honoring the tribune of conservatism, Robert Taft, on their way to proclaim unalterable dedication to those conservative principles that Taft had steadfastly observed, only to act in agreement with "liberal" colleagues whose ideology they condemn with ferocity when elections approach. Their rhetoric is hypocritical, contrived to deceive opponents and please supporters. Their "conservatism" is merely a conceit, a pretense to link them with conservative traditions which they have abandoned. The reality behind the mask of rhetorical banalities—the strident calls to reduce expenditures and "balance the budget"—is that "conservatives" have joined with many of their "liberal" colleagues to become the biggest spenders in the nation's history. And they have willingly led government into the arena of private enterprise wherever profits are to be protected or private failures compensated from the public treasury.

Contemporary rhetorical debate, as befits our more bureaucratic age, centers on the desirability of a national industrial policy. This is nothing more than a change of slogans. Interference has been ennobled with a phrase more suited to academic discourse. The result, as always, is simply to confuse discussion. We already have an industrial policy, just as government "interference" was always essential to democratic capitalism. The issue is not the existence of an industrial policy, but the wisdom of its goals and conduct.

For there is no such thing as business exempt from government interference (or industrial policy) and there never has been. During every significant period in American history, the dominant economic structures have been drastically different from earlier ones. Some changes were a natural evolution; many were the result of popular demand and the actions of political leadership. Even before America became a nation, the Constitutional Convention was convoked for the purpose of modifying interstate economic barriers, which were crippling commerce and national growth. Once assembled, the delegates went far beyond their original mandate. Instead of modifying the laws of the states, they united them in a new country. But the originating purpose was economic: to increase the flow of commerce by shaping a competitive market that would be national in scale, but was then fragmented by the diverse regulations and powers of thirteen semi-independent states.

From our earliest years to the present, the corridors of private commerce—bridges and canals, railroads and highways, airfields and aircraft—have largely been the work of government. Many private individuals were enriched in the process and large fortunes were made. But the direction came from government, and the capital came from the taxpayers. Nor could it have been otherwise. For individual enterprises could not have paid such huge sums. Yet they were beneficiaries, as was the nation, of government intervention to supply the foundation of capitalism.

Charles Carroll of Carrollton, the last survivor of those who had signed our Declaration of Independence, lifted the first spade of earth for the construction of the Baltimore and Ohio Railway; his presence was intended to link the principles of our creation with the growth of enterprise. Commerce could give content to opportunity. The President at that time was Andrew Jackson, who acted to destroy the virtually autonomous Bank of the United States, which had almost unrestrained power over the nation's currency and credit. Unmoved by protests and organized objections from our most powerful financial interests, which regarded the bank as a pillar of the capitalist system and protection against the potential irrationalities of democratic rule, Jackson mounted his assault. Yet the ultimate result, after a somewhat rocky interlude, was to reduce the power of a small group of Eastern financiers to dominate the flow of capital, to expand the supply of currency and credit to the developing West, to strengthen and multiply independent financial institutions, and to facilitate the flow of commerce across a growing nation. Jackson's successful action provided new room for the growth of capitalism.

In the middle of the Civil War, Lincoln established the land-grant colleges, which brought education to the pioneers and would lead to an explosion in agriculture; at the same time, he journeyed to the Far West to observe the construction of the transcontinental railroad, a project built so that business could flourish in a market that now spanned a continent. Even while the Union was divided in bloody conflict, links to strengthen it were being completed.

As America's industrial power grew, government was called upon to halt business abuse and stimulate economic activity. Laws were passed to outlaw large concentrations of business, which threatened to control the marketplace in order to eliminate the competition essential to free enterprise. Such laws were supported by many businesses whose survival was threatened, although unfortunately they did little damage to the monopolies and trusts. In fact, twenty-five new trusts were formed within five years after passage of the Sherman Antitrust Act. Under Woodrow Wilson we established a Federal Trade Commission empowered to prevent unfair competition, a law supported by many businesses, which felt threatened by larger and more voracious competitors.

Government has also acted to strengthen our financial institutions, making it easier for business to obtain capital for investment. It has intervened to compel banks to extend credit for agriculture and new enterprise. By insuring deposits, it largely prevented the destructive bank panics that had often injured, sometimes crippled, economic activity. (But lawmakers did not foresee the contemporary use of deposit insurance as a lever to obtain funds for reckless speculation.)

No method of social surgery, however sophisticated and advanced it may become, can ever separate government from private business or abolish a government industrial policy. It is both impossible and undesirable to do so. Indeed, were government to announce that all federal "interference" with business was to be halted tonight, the entire economy would collapse by tomorrow morning.

The corporation begins its life as a creation of the state, given flesh by legal charters that circumscribe its powers and activities. The entire structure of business and production, our machinery for the creation of wealth, is entangled in a gigantic net of laws, agencies, and regulations: securities laws and tax laws; antitrust prohibitions and agricultural subsidies; bureaucratic rules, presidential directives, and legislative demands. Every day of every week a highly paid army of lawyers and accountants and lobbyists toils to direct the multitudinous interventions of government toward the desires of their private employers.

The strong and inescapable relation between business and government is heightened by the fact that our monstrous Washington bureaucracies, the elected and the appointed, buy about 20 percent of all the goods and services produced by the nation. These bureaucrats' decisions on how to spend this money and where can bring huge profits to some industries, speed others along the path to collapse.

Democratic government and private enterprise are intimately, irrevocably interfused, the heartbeat and arteries of the nation. The American system is not simply capitalism, but *democratic* capitalism: the power of property subject to the power of the people. Therefore, the issue is not the desirability of government "interference," but the uses, ends, and moral values toward which it should be directed— to benefit the nation or enrich the few.

Our concern is not to protect industry from its own folly. If the incapacities of economic bureaucracy brought down a company or two, the loss could be regarded as a natural result of failure in the competitive struggle. But not when mammoth industries that dominate the entire American economy are damaged. When enormous size—and the now distorted anatomy of size—results in inefficiency, stagnation of productivity, a lessening of our competitive ability, a decline in income and employment, and the spread of poverty, then it strikes at the well-being and greatness of America itself.

Were the producers of steel or automobiles or consumer electronics subject to election, they would long since have been driven from office. But size and concentrated wealth—however incompetently managed—are a source of immense power within society. That power has been able to corrupt the political process, but it cannot guarantee increased productivity, national growth, or economic justice. Indeed, it often has little interest in such national objectives, preferring to exercise its influence to attain its own short-term goals. When the objectives of the custodians of private wealth can prevail over the needs of the citizenry, then the well-being and future greatness of America are in danger. If the wealthy are able to corrupt the political process, and to assert their demands over the most pressing needs of the country, then the futures of all Americans are in danger.

And we have gone a very long way down that road. Causes of distress so deeply embedded in the foundation cannot easily be transformed. But they are, we must remember, the creation of human error and human failure. Since, therefore, they are practical problems, they have practical solutions. Change and restoration, however, cannot be rhetorically summoned into existence, materialized by appeals to patriotism. It is not enough to love America, or to ask for God's blessing. We all love this country, and with sincerity at least equal to that of any politician, we can ask that "God bless America." But neither love nor God will change the ominous direction of American life. That is a difficult job for an angry and justly aggrieved people.

I offer no comprehensive agenda for the reversal of decline. I do, however, have some specific and tangible suggestions for such an agenda, preliminary steps toward the formation of a movement for democratic capitalism. Conventional remedies, such as tinkering with the tax code or transferring money between programs, although they may confer some benefit, are inadequate to the underlying sources of decline, which are now embedded in the "system" itself. For this reason, the proposals are directed solely at important changes in the economic structure that now dominates much of American life. We have made changes of similar intent and magnitude before. Indeed, American history has involved a constant restructuring designed to preserve essential principles against the assaults of shifting circumstance. One thinks, for example, of labor's fierce struggle for the right to organize, or African-Americans' battle to eliminate legalized segregation. Although not without turbulence and occasional violence, with the exception of the Civil War, we have been able to meet such challenges within the ruling constitutional framework.

Any agenda for economic change must, at a minimum, respond to five significant deficiencies in today's democratic capitalism. First, to reduce or eliminate the bureaucratization that has lessened the ability of some important industries to compete. Second, to stimulate investment in America and protect businesses—established or newly conceived—that seek to create wealth through competitive success in any market of the world. Third, to convert to civilian production the military industries and technological abilities established for defense against the now moribund Soviet Union. Fourth, to ensure economic justice by expanding the market to extend opportunity to those now excluded (particularly people of color), and to eliminate the maldistribution of income that has already reduced consumption and impaired the nation's growth. (It may be recalled that the maldistribution of personal income during the 1920s was a significant cause of the Depression of the 1930s. We are already approaching distortions of comparable magnitude.) Fifth, to educate our working population and equip it with the information and skills necessary for today's increasingly sophisticated processes of production.

REDUCING BUREAUCRACY

All markets are established by the legal order. There is scarcely any commercial transaction that is not shaped and governed by law, whether it be a government requirement to test the safety of new drugs or the anciently rooted principles that determine the existence and validity of a contract. The conduct of business is made possible by the existence, at state and federal levels, of compendious commercial codes and the common law of commerce. Since the law defines the market, such markets are free in the sense that a person can choose his own government as long as he votes for the Democratic or Republican presidential candidate. Within the historical experience of advanced societies, all forms of control over the modern market have evolved toward bureaucracy, leading to enlarged concentrations that extend and accelerate that bureaucratization.

Just such a process was occurring, concealed beneath the surface of mounting affluence, as postwar growth enlarged the possibilities for larger and more powerful concentrations with increased ability to control the market. The consequent movement toward bureaucratic organization diminished the capacity of our industry to compete in today's market, and has limited its ability to adapt swiftly to a future whose only certainty is technological innovation, changing markets, intensification of competition, and the emergence of new competitors. (Ironically, the entrance of foreign competitors, in creating a market that could not be controlled, illuminated the deepening deficiencies of American business which would inevitably reduce our growth in the long run. And the success of those same competitors now serves to stimulate change. This stimulus, unfortunately, has come at a very high price.)

One cannot, of course, compel those who control private business to take measures that will enable them to succeed in the market. Conduct of their businesses is in their hands. They alone can make the decisions to modernize or increase efficiency, or reduce unproductive costs. (After a decade of competition and steadily decreasing market share, our automobile companies have been unable to match the efficiency, ingenuity, and marketing skills of their Japanese competitors. Japanese car production is not a military secret. We know what they do. We just don't do it, much less make improvements of our own. The recent history of our automobile industry is a case study in the bureaucratization of industry.)

It is, however, possible to require changes in corporate structure and practice that will make it advantageous to devote resources and energy to building a company capable of adapting to changing circumstances, and to reach a level of efficiency that will allow the most productive use of resources. Our economy already contains incentives to change. Future growth and profits are among them, and the ultimate incentive is failure. As the current conduct of American industry demonstrates, such incentives are inadequate.

A tax on nonreinvested profits should be imposed. This tax would be an effective incentive for business to modernize and expand, thus increasing its competitive abilities. (The Japanese spend twice as much as we do on the modernization of industry.) It would diminish the temptation to divert resources to the enrichment of executives and shareholders or to uneconomic acquisitions. At the same time, by increasing the value of the business the tax would add to prospects for a renewal of growth. This tax is somewhat like the investment tax credit, except that instead of paying business to invest, business would be charged for not investing—a considerable gain to the taxpayer and the federal budget.

With the subservient acquiescence of carefully handpicked directors, some managers whose market share and earnings are actually declining do not hesitate to vote themselves increased compensation, amounting to many millions of dollars, drawn from the assets of the company. For them, the immediate economic rewards that can be extracted from failure are more important than the more speculative rewards of future success. Obviously this fact adversely influences their management of the company.

Executive compensation should be linked to the actual economic performance of a company. Thus success will be rewarded and failure penalized—a fundamental, but frequently violated, tenet of capitalist enterprise. Once compensation and promotion are closely tied to competitive success—as reflected by increased market share and the prospect of rising earnings—the pressure to eliminate bureaucratic restraints (that is, to violate the norms of "corporate culture") will be greatly intensified. One would like to believe that most managers will take such actions, not because doing so will reward them better, but for "the good of the company." But that is less likely than the prospect that people will act in ways consistent with Lincoln's cynical observation that all "mankind in the past, present and future in all their actions are moved and controlled by a motive, and, at bottom, the snaky tongue of selfishness will wag out."

Since, in most companies, shareholders—the nominal owners—now have little voice in establishing executive compensation, it will be necessary to change corporate law in order to establish general guidelines and to require shareholder ratification of payments to executives, along with the right to initiate a process of reduction. Steve Ross may no longer receive an annual pay envelope containing $39 million to preside over the shaky fortunes of Time Warner. But those who add to production and increase the ability to compete will be paid in some rough proportion to their achievements.

Workers should be allowed significant participation in management decisions. Of the three groups that nominally determine the fate of an enterprise, managers and shareholders come and go, rewarded—if blessed by good fortune—for their efforts; workers alone are tied to the long-term fortunes of the enterprise. Failure can reduce their income and standard of living. For many it can mean the loss of jobs, reduction to poverty, dependence on pitifully small government handouts. Their entire way of life is at stake. Those who may be called upon to make the largest sacrifice for failure deserve to be heard when vital decisions are made.

Nor is fairness the only benefit. Workers who are allowed to participate in decisions will increase their understanding of the needs and problems of the company. This may well make labor negotiations easier. It will certainly enhance worker identification with the fortunes of the company, and probably strengthen the so-called work ethic, whose decay is bemoaned at every gathering of the managerial class.

American values and culture are very different from those of Japan or Germany. American workers do not want company T-shirts, group calisthenics, or a morning rendition of the company anthem. They will respond, not to symbols of an imaginary brotherhood, but to participation and responsibility, which is not company hype but a reality, and one that allows them to share in the judgments that will shape their future. This attitude and sensibility are built into the American character.

During the Second World War, American workers were joined in a common endeavor against a common enemy. They had a personal stake in the quality and volume of production. They became the most productive work force in the world, far outdoing the laborers of Japan and Germany combined. Of course, the struggle to enhance the fortunes of a single enterprise is not a war. Yet there is some similarity. An external threat to the quality of workers' lives can be seen as precipitating a struggle whose successful outcome will enhance their future. Participation can help to blend these realities into a cause. And should American workers be allowed to participate in the leadership of such a cause, they will demonstrate that they remain the best and most creative in the world.

Laws should be enacted to prohibit uneconomic mergers, acquisitions, and leveraged buyouts. We have seen that in recent years companies and groups of investors borrowed vast amounts of capital to buy other companies, or to buy up stock in their own company, thus replacing equity with debt. Although the deal-makers got rich, the companies and the economy often did not do as well. The burden of large and expensive debt lessened the ability of many companies to function profitably, deprived others of resources necessary to modernize and finance product innovation, and in some cases precipitated destruction.

Such financial machinations must be prohibited. No company should be sold to another, or to its own management,

without first proving that the American economy will benefit. A demonstrated likelihood of increased production and
enhanced productivity should be required. Undoubtedly,
the laws and regulations needed to enforce such a prohibition would be complex and difficult to draft, but no more
so than current regulation of the securities and banking
industries. Such a prohibition would extend the philosophy
of the antitrust laws—the protection of a competitive market from the power of finance—to more recent and differently contrived techniques of manipulation.

STIMULATING INVESTMENT

A national effort to revitalize the American economy will
require federal spending. But not all spending is the same.
Some federal expenditures—either direct or in the form of
tax cuts—are designed for immediate consumption; these
expenditures range from the multiplying costs of government itself to providing food stamps for 23 million of our
impoverished citizens. When the government repairs a
decaying interstate highway or finances the development of
new technology, however, it is making an investment that
is intended to bring increased productivity and an incremen-
tal rise in national wealth. The distinction between consumption in the present and investment in the future is
self-evident. Yet the federal budget fails to make any distinction. Politicians are tempted to reduce or postpone productive—and often urgently needed—investment in order to
gratify more immediate needs. And few have resisted temptation.

Walt W. Rostow has proposed that we "split the federal
budget between capital and current expenditures as do more

than forty states and virtually all other industrial countries." Revising the structure of the budget will not itself reduce the federal deficit. That will require far more draconian measures by a changed government which functions in the service of the people. But splitting the budget is more than mere creative accounting. Rostow reminds us that we have "been living off capital for ten years." Unless we are willing to repair the decay of a decade, and at the same time divert additional resources to new sources of growth, decline will continue and even accelerate. Publicly identifying productive federal investments designed, in Rostow's words, to "trigger the economy back to a sustained general revival" may help mobilize the far larger effort at restoration, which will require change and sacrifice by private businesses and individual citizens alike.

The most obvious candidate for inclusion in Rostow's capital budget are the resources to build and restore the basic material framework for the conduct of commerce on a continental—now global—scale, which is customarily called the infrastructure. National growth required a continental system of transportation—canals, railroads, highways; these are still essential, but rapidly deteriorating. However, the composition of infrastructure is always changing. No government or entrepreneur would undertake the reconstruction of the Erie Canal today, except perhaps as a theme park, and the Pony Express exists only as a nostalgic ghost floating wistfully through the American memory.

A similar change in the composition of infrastructure has come to the modern economy. Technology and information have become the crucial elements of today's infrastructure, the emerging weapons of successful competition. This is a change we should welcome. But unfortunately, much of our unmatched technical skill—the sophisticated capacities descended from the legendary Yankee tinkerer through Edison and Ford—has been lavished on military projects that have contributed little to long-term growth.

It took us only a few years to transform a handful of mathematical formulas into the most powerful destructive weapon ever conceived. Our air force developed and tested aircraft that in private hands dominated the aerospace market of the world. Many important advances in electronic technology emerged from the defense and space programs. But the research that produced such technological triumphs—even when conducted through private companies—was financed by the government. Some of the advances it produced—such as advanced semiconductors, lasers, and jet aircraft—had important potential applications for consumer products. But, unfortunately, many of our businesses, immobilized by bureaucratic caution, managed by financial experts, with engineers and production experts omitted from the ranks of decision-makers, failed to pursue the potential for profitable commercial innovation in the creations of our scientists. Others did not make the same mistake.

Outside the military industry, as a result of what must be the all-time champion of false economies, we have cut back on basic scientific research. And we have directed a great deal of our native ingenuity toward the creation of new technology for its own sake, not as a means of excelling in the competitive marketplace. Our competitors have proven the opportunity was there. Many of our more recent inventions—in optics, semiconductors, computer chips, and the like—were utilized by others to create profitable consumer products. And although we invented the ubiquitous and multifunctional microprocessor, the Japanese now control 50 percent of the world's production.

Research, like railroads and highways, is expensive. Its

results are often unforeseeable and therefore incalculable. Some smaller companies have made important advances, especially in new products that can be made for a relatively small market. But research directed at industrial production, its economic benefits inherently speculative, necessarily conducted on a large scale, is beyond the means of all but the largest private businesses. And many of these, immobilized by a stagnating corporate culture, have failed to pursue innovation.

Such limits on the resources and capacity of private business are the familiar attributes of traditional infrastructure projects. There is, however, an important difference. If the government builds a road it is highly unlikely that a competitor will lay down a parallel highway in hopes of attracting profitable traffic. But the technological infrastructure is intensely competitive. Laboratories on three continents are seeking an advantage in the technology of the future—for example, by pursuing high-definition television, automating production, improving product design, advancing optical communications, and much more. This makes our own effort far more urgent and any further waste of our own abilities inexcusable. Therefore:

The government should establish a series of advanced, highly sophisticated centers to develop technology for the shifting needs, fashions, and desires of the civilian market. Such centers would conduct research and pursue invention. But they would also work to transform invention into consumer products and into improvements in the process of production, from robotic assembly to techniques of cost reduction. One cannot foresee what creations would emerge. That is best left to science-fiction writers and the imagination of nonfiction scientists. Experience, however, has taught us that the possibilities are large and failure to pursue them is costly. The creations of such government research centers would be made freely available—without patent restrictions—to any American entrepreneur willing to invest in production and marketing. The agency responsible for administering these centers would also contain a separate staff of technically sophisticated people who would actively consult with smaller businesses.

In the future as in the past, the great majority of new jobs will be created not by titanic enterprises but through America's abundance of small businesses. Yet many small-business people are unlikely to realize that some technological advances, originated for other purposes, might be applied to increase their own profitability. Improvements in production processes, for example, which have been designed for large industrial enterprises, might well be scaled down to the needs of a small machine shop. It would be part of government's job not only to develop technological innovations, but to market them to enterprises unequipped to follow and evaluate the potential value of scientific advances. In this age of science, many of us are still technologically illiterate. An individual unable to program a video recorder, for instance, is unlikely to glimpse the potential business benefits of laser technology.

We know we can make smart bombs. We can also, if we mobilize and support our talent, make a dishwasher that actually cleans dishes, build a toaster whose every aspect is perfection, design better ways to reproduce music or guide an automobile to its destination. In fact, we have already done some of these things, yet the products which incorporate our ideas bear the label "Sanyo" or "Krups." No nation can match America's capacity for invention. But jobs, increased income, a higher standard of living, pride in economic success do not come from invention. They depend upon using invention to create, package, and market products that people want to buy.

Direct incentives in the form of guaranteed loans, tax credits, and even an occasional subsidy for modernization should be provided to those smaller entrepreneurs who find access to capital increasingly difficult. (In this context the word "modernization" implies all measures designed to increase the competitive strength of a business enterprise, from installing new machinery to training a sales force in foreign languages and customs.) Such direct assistance will be offered only for a relatively short term and only to businesses that allocate it to approved plans. (During the Depression, the newly established Reconstruction Finance Corporation made loans amounting to many billions of dollars to assist businesses in distress. Ultimately it recovered all of its money, and even made a profit for the Treasury.) It is unfortunate that this program might require the creation of another government bureaucracy, an objection somewhat diluted by the condition that assistance be limited to programs devised by the company itself and rationally related to modernization.

Loan capital should be made available to larger businesses and to promising new enterprises. As we have seen, the instruments of today's capital market—thrifts, banks, even foreign investors—have been compelled to refrain from all but the most conservative loans. We have described the immense waste and reckless extravagance of two decades which choked the channels of investment and seriously wounded our entire financial structure, crippling the ability of established enterprises to modernize and expand. If our large automobile companies complain that they are unable to secure investment capital, how can lesser industries expect to acquire the funds essential to rebuild their competitive position? Yet access to capital is the fuel of enterprise. One does not build something from nothing. If private institutions cannot or will not meet the need, government must. Of course there is some risk. Risk is inherent in the nature of capitalism. However, if we wish to enlarge our capacity to create wealth for the nation, someone, some instrument of finance, must be willing to gamble, to provide resources for an investment program that shows potential for profit. And as private sources shrivel or withdraw, only the government is left. We have done it before; Washington moved decisively to prevent the collapse of the Chrysler Corporation, for example. And we still do it for some segments of the economy, such as agriculture. If we are unwilling to expand public participation in the capital market, it will not be possible to revitalize private enterprise.

The federal budget deficit should be eliminated. Few measures would do more to improve our long-run ability to compete. Except in time of war or other national emergency, a balanced federal budget should be mandated, either by statute or by constitutional amendment. Although a legal prohibition on deficit spending is theoretically possible, the only realistic approach is through constitutional amendment. No law will be able to withstand the assaults of a parochial and extravagant Congress.

In the past, deficit spending, though often criticized, has been of little harm and less public concern. But, like the crew of the starship *Enterprise,* we've been carried by a sudden shift into warp speed into an entirely new galaxy of debt. In order to avoid raising taxes, we have borrowed a great deal of money. We owe more than $4 trillion, and we continue to borrow. Annual interest payments now are the largest single component of the federal budget, diverting a great deal of money (more than $300 billion, and rising) from public needs to private borrowers.

In more frugal and hopeful times, we were often advised that the federal debt was not a serious concern. After all, we owed the money to ourselves, and repayment would ultimately reenter the American economy. That is no longer true. Unable to finance our own debt, we have turned to foreign lenders. Thus, some of the wealth used for repayment, and for a portion of current interest, will leave America for other lands. Some of it may be used to buy American businesses. Some may be used to expand enterprise in Kyoto or Stuttgart. As a result, the deficit now exacerbates our shortage of investment capital, and thus increases the difficulty of reversing economic decline. Yet, year after year Congress and the President blithely propose and enact deficits equal in magnitude to those which have already transformed us into the world's largest borrower. We must bite the bullet now and force ourselves to live within our means. It won't be easy, and it will require sacrifice. But a failure to sacrifice now will, inevitably, place far larger and more damaging burdens on a future that is fast approaching.

The government should provide temporary protection against foreign competition to those American businesses that have failed to meet the skilled and vigorous challenges of foreign competition, whether through managerial shortsightedness or through an inability to foresee the swift evolution of the modern economy.

Such protection can take many forms: tariffs, quotas, subsidies, or outright prohibitions. Such protective measures are not intended as a wall to shield American business against its own inefficiencies and failures. They merely acknowledge the reality that we have fallen behind in many areas of enterprise, under an assault that came unexpectedly and with unanticipated force. We need time to regain our competitive momentum. It is a chance to catch up, and will advantage only those who use that chance, not for short-term gain, but to prepare to compete in an open world market. Such protections will be limited to a realistically specific period of time. They would be offered only to those industries willing to prepare and pursue a program of modernization designed to make them fully competitive. (The near collapse of the American motorcycle industry stimulated just such an approach. As a result the Harley-Davidson company has moved from the edge of bankruptcy to a prosperous and respected place in the market.)

It is our own fault that foreign competitors have surpassed us in many areas of enterprise. But the question is not a moral one. The creation of wealth for the nation—the standard of American life—depends upon our capacity to regain a competitive advantage. Because it is vital to the welfare of our people and country, and not from sympathy for our own myopic businesses, we must at least give American enterprise this chance to show what it can do. In the long run, of course, there is no escape from the rigors of a world market. Global economic ties are already too strong and too extensive. The winds of change are already risen, and no barrier can wall out the wind.

But there is nothing wrong with protection, especially when it is temporary, and if what you are protecting is yourself. Nor should we fear a trade war, that menacing incantation of those who believe—whether from self-interest or ideological dogma—that the American market should be a freely available source of enriching profits for the people of every land. Not that there is much chance of a trade war. For the very failures of our own industries, which have increased our demand for foreign products, mean that potential adversaries would have a great deal to lose. We are, after all, our competitors' most important foreign market.

But should such peaceful conflict arise, we are still very strong, with the largest and richest domestic market in the world. We can hold our own. If our legitimate effort to rebuild our economy does create a certain amount of strife, it will only compel us to work harder. Moreover, a hard-fought contest has always been good for the American spirit.

Many people, including many Americans, have accumulated riches and political power derived from participation in the foreign incursions that have transferred American resources to other countries. They have a great deal of influence, and they employ a phalanx of economists to chant the exorcising mantra "free trade" and thus ward off the slightest sign of support for demonic "protectionism." But there is no mystical power or cryptic talisman hidden in those words. Free trade is not free. Not to the workers who lose their jobs, or to businessmen who lose their customers, or to enterprises that are forced into bankruptcy, or to entire industries that—like consumer electronics—are swept from the face of the continent.

Protectionism in this form is not like the sweeping tariff bills of earlier times. It is selective, limited in time, contingent upon implementing a program of modernization. It simply recognizes the past inadequacies that have cost the country so dearly, and gives business time to prepare a remedy before the gates are lifted. At one time this concept was invoked in America to nurture the growth of "infant industries." It can now be applied, with equal justice, to speed the recovery of injured industries—whether they are victims of assaults by others or of their own clumsy self-mutilations. It does not matter who is to blame. It is only important that their health be restored.

In addition to conditional protection for American-owned businesses, we should limit foreign acquisition of American commercial assets. We have examined the danger to the American future that is inherent in the sale of American businesses to foreign purchasers. If we allow others to buy our productive assets, the businesses may remain in America, but the wealth they create will increase growth, income, and opportunity for others. (That's why they bought them in the first place.) In a few industries, deemed to be especially strategic (such as airlines), we already limit foreign investment. But, for the most part, American assets are for sale to anyone with the money. And what foreigners are buying is our future.

A special commission should be established and directed—subject to public debate and congressional approval—to set limits and guidelines for foreign acquisitions. No substantial sale of American property to foreign owners should be allowed until that commission certifies that the proposed transaction both satisfies the guidelines and is in our national interest. Few American businessmen are so patriotic that they will refuse an offer from foreign sources if the price is high enough. That judgment should be reserved to those whose principal obligation is to the country and its people.

BEATING SWORDS INTO PLOWSHARES

For many years, critical authorities like Seymour Melman and Lloyd Dumas have demonstrated the debilitating impact of defense spending on the civilian economy and urged America to develop a program for a time when events would allow the conversion of military industry to civilian needs. That time has now come. It is self-evident that the nation needs, and quickly, a plan to turn military industry and talent toward fully modernized civilian production. For more than forty years the military has required resources so vast that their value exceeded the fixed, reproducible, tangible wealth of the entire civilian economy. Had the expense of defense been less, some of that money could have been used to strengthen our declining civilian economy. Much might have gone to reduce the huge burden of national debt which now obstructs every measure to heal the country's afflictions.

Equally damaging to our economic strength, perhaps more so, was the diversion of about 30 percent of our limited pool of scientific talent from civilian needs. One can always borrow, or print, more money. But neither the President nor the Congress can appropriate more scientists or engineers than we possess. Yet success in a modern, competitive economy depends on such skills, and we have undoubtedly paid a price for their dedication to military needs. Our near abandonment of the consumer electronics industry, for example, came about largely because our unmatched technological capacities were focused on the preparations necessary for war. Large electronics companies found it more profitable to employ the scientifically skilled to build smart bombs, or more precise nuclear weapons, than to manufacture VCRs, television sets, or display screens for portable computers.

Naturally, the needs of national security come first. I am not suggesting that we should have made a different use of the resources and talent that we drew upon to protect our freedom and the independence of much of the world during the half-century of the Cold War. (Although we might have sought a closer relationship between the money we spent and the value we received.) The Soviet threat was real enough. As an advisor to President Kennedy, I lived through some of it—those tense days in the White House when we prepared to use tanks and troops to force our way through a threatened obstruction of the corridor to Berlin, or the fearful, silent waiting as Soviet ships approached our blockade of Cuba during the Missile Crisis of 1962.

But in the last few years, with almost miraculous dispatch, the Soviet empire has collapsed, and its feared military machine no longer threatens destruction of the West. It will be a long time before historians can sort out the reasons for such transforming events. But surely among them will be the policy of military deterrence which was the foundation of our defense program. (We might also discover that the Soviet Union spent itself into bankruptcy while we merely spent ourselves into a recession.)

The Soviet danger was unique, capable of devastating our entire society within a single hour. It was this nuclear threat, not the sheer size of the Soviet military machine, that required that we maintain a large defense establishment prepared for immediate action. The dissolution of that danger means we can make large reductions in defense spending without endangering our national security. At least, we can if the military-industrial complex has not become so powerful that it will be allowed to spend the hundreds of billions once directed at the Soviet threat to secure us against the limitless possibilities of danger that the wizards of the Pentagon are capable of conjuring. (One can, of course, conjure up any conceivable scenario, no matter how farfetched, whether it be a Mexican invasion, an insurgency of American Indians, or the need for force to settle conflicts in Azerbaijan, the Balkans, or Peru.)

The reality, however, is that there are no new threats—at least none of large dimension and presenting the possibility of immediate and widespread destruction. Undoubtedly, the future will bring new dangers. But if and when they come, we will have had time to prepare. And we will be able to prepare better and more swiftly if our efforts are founded on a healthy civilian economy and a people united in spirit and principle. It is our people, their work and their beliefs, and not our missile-guidance systems or bombs of uncommon intelligence that are the only secure foundation of our national security. And they have proven it in many ways over two centuries.

"What constitutes the bulwark of our own liberty and independence?" Lincoln asked. "It is not our frowning battlements, our bristling sea coasts, our army and our navy. . . . Our reliance is in the love of liberty. . . . Our defense is in the spirit which prized liberty as the heritage of all men." The rebuilding of America is, at bottom, the strengthening of that liberty on which our national security depends. The end of the Cold War should be viewed as an enormous and unexpected opportunity to increase the strength of that liberty, freeing our huge military industry to pursue the creation of national wealth and increased individual prosperity. Obviously, industries and workers now engaged in military work are concerned about their future. Their anxiety is understandable. But it should not be justified. They are badly needed.

There is a great deal of work to be done in an America moving through recession, threatened by depression. Highly developed industries, a multitude of talented individuals, and some of the best research laboratories in the world will now be available to aid in the restoration of America. One can glean some slight hint of possibilities from the use by foreign competitors of scientific advances, originated by American military or space research, to create some of those consumer products and production techniques that have allowed them to surpass us.

The transition from military to civilian production will not be easy. One cannot simply cut military spending and expect a smooth and rapid flow of resources, industries, and laboratories to civilian production. One does not easily transform an industry that not only is enormous in scale, but has not been compelled to develop many of the abilities necessary for success in the competitive civilian market. About 6.5 million people now work in the armed forces, at the Pentagon, and in military industry. Many of our most advanced research laboratories are almost wholly devoted to defense work. The Pentagon's central office is probably the largest bureaucracy in the world, and it controls the largest bloc of finance capital available to any American management. Transforming any substantial portion of so extensive an enterprise is an almost Sisyphean labor.

Yet an even greater difficulty is the fact that military industries have not operated in anything like a free-market environment. They had only one important "customer." (And a few small ones on other continents.) Nearly all their competition—to the extent there was any at all—was with a handful of American businesses. The cost discipline, agile adaptation to changing consumer demand, and methods of penetrating a variety of markets which are all necessary to civilian competition have been largely absent from the military industry.

If we are to prepare military industries and scientific talent for competitive success, some form of planned conversion is essential. A variety of such plans has already been proposed. Their comparative merits can be debated at great length. However, it is critically important that we do have a plan, and not abandon the process to chance. Under government sponsorship, conversion plans for individual industries or research centers should be drafted by individuals of proven business skill, assigned to work with current managers or owners, not with government bureaucrats. Except for some federal facilities, most of the military industry is privately owned and managed, and can best be prepared for competition in the civilian market with help from those whose understanding has been confirmed by commercial success. The government would, however, retain responsibility for ensuring that a plan is prepared and implementation begun. If the changeover is conducted wisely and at a moderate pace, reduced military spending will prove to be an enormous benefit to America, allowing us to transform the wondrous facilities and unmatched talent of our military establishment into an instrument of raw economic power.

ENSURING ECONOMIC JUSTICE

Measures to help correct the depression-threatening maldistribution of income are necessary to restore economic justice. The tax codes of recent years are a modern confirmation of Madison's observation that there is no power of government other than the "apportionment of taxes . . . in which greater opportunity and temptation are given to a predominant party to trample on the rules of justice. It is vain to say enlightened statesmen will be able to adjust these clashing interests and render them all subservient to the public good. Enlightened statesmen will not always be at the helm." Laws that have increased the taxes on working Americans (the 60 percent who constitute the middle class) while lowering taxes on the wealthy prove how sorely we want for "enlightened statesmen."

The tax code should be thoroughly revised to restore fairness and simplicity, guided, perhaps, by the precept of Alexander Hamilton—a conservative leader, contemptuous of the people and an opponent of their power—who nonetheless enjoined the national administration "to go as far as may be practicable in making the luxury of the rich tributary to the public treasury."

Some of the abuses that have transferred wealth upward—the enormous profits made from unproductive deals, the ingenious financial manipulations, the government subsidies to favored interests, the waste and deliberate misuse of federal expenditures that have enriched the privileged— could all be eliminated by a combination of legislation and intensified oversight by Congress and the agencies it has spawned to help regulate the economy. Reform and rigorous regulation of the banking system could halt accumulation of wealth by those who have benefited from the lavish and reckless speculation of our financial institutions. "I fear banking establishments even more than standing armies," Jefferson wrote. And he was not a timid man. Unfortunately it would constitute an abandonment of reason to expect the same government that conspired in these abuses to now correct them, and to turn against the very interests that have so lavishly suborned it. Although economic justice is among the fundamental principles of American democracy, its restoration will have to await the restoration of the democratic process.

A great deal of wealth unrelated to productive enterprise has been acquired by those skilled enough to master a simple formula: Loot the Treasury, con the banks, and stay out of jail. There were many, now comfortably enjoying the fruits of their success, who did just that. And one must admit that the temptations were great. For the guardians of the Treasury often neglected to lock the vaults, while many bankers eagerly gave their depositors' money to almost anyone who arrived in an Armani suit, carrying a proposal so skillfully contrived and documented that it might have spurred Indiana Jones into action.

Structural changes to ensure fairness are easier to describe than to accomplish. In the secrecy of legislative chambers, powerful opposition will make its appearance, composed of the beneficiaries of present injustice and their allies in government. But the lawful power to make the changes is there, and they are essential to enlarging the market on which economic growth depends.

Yet fairness alone is not enough. The equitable distribution of decline does not increase prosperity. It was not merely justice but twenty-five years of rising personal income that made America prosperous. The creation of wealth combined with fair distribution is the only path to a renewed rise in personal income. It will not be achieved by giving small, temporary tax cuts (handouts) to a middle class already deeply in debt and living on the edge. Nor will it come from a sudden increase in consumption. For only after personal income rises, and workers feel secure in their employment, will consumers spend as they once did. Nor should we expect them to. Often they don't have the money. And, even if they do, these are uncertain times. Men and women are being laid off. Income is tight. They have borrowed a lot of money. The economic future is uncertain. Better to leave money in the bank for a while, or pay down the credit card. Under such conditions it is a fantasy to anticipate individuals and families, well supplied with cash and credit cards, suddenly flooding the malls to indulge an unconsummated desire for consumer goods. After all, the stores will still be open next week, next month, or next year. Maybe.

During his third term, Roosevelt proposed an economic bill of rights. First among them was a right to "remunerative jobs." Exercise of this right is the only way to increase personal income. But a right that cannot be used is not a right at all, it is merely a hope. One cannot exercise a right to jobs that do not exist, or to compensation that business cannot or will not provide. Can a right of access to remunerative jobs be secured? Only if we rebuild our industrial structure and equip our people with the skills it will require.

Only a thriving economy, fully competitive with its rivals, can provide the American majority with rising income and economic security. There is no shortcut.

No effort to arrest and reverse national decline can succeed until we incorporate the impoverished and disfranchised into the larger society. Poverty has removed many millions of our people from participation in the national economy, none more decisively or irrevocably than the residents of our inner cities, especially the young who have abandoned the values and aspirations that are part of our American heritage. Instead of helping to create wealth, they have become a drain on our resources—not only directly, through welfare programs, but in the large and incalculable costs of illness, crime, drugs, and despoliation of the urban environment. If any substantial fraction of these abandoned Americans can be rescued, the entire economy will be strengthened. The prosperity and growth of our economy depend on mass consumption. Yet only those who perform relatively skilled work can afford to consume. It is ironic, although a truism, that if the number of idle poor decline, the income of the rich will rise.

In the early 1960s, when President Johnson announced his national "War on Poverty," victory seemed possible. The poor were fewer and more widely dispersed. The economy was in a period of sustained growth and, amid this abundance, there was a growing consensus that the elimination of poverty was a national responsibility whose fulfillment was within our means. These conditions no longer exist. Johnson's War on Poverty was not confined to blacks. It embraced the millions of white and Hispanic and Asian Americans who live in exile within their own country. It was, while it lasted, not merely an economic program, but a gloriously ambitious attempt to reconfirm the seminal ideal of America as a community with shared beliefs, goals, and responsibilities.

But the War on Poverty is dead. Instead, from the inner recesses of the White House and from some presidential campaign headquarters, there is issuing a deliberate effort to win votes by arousing the very fears that Johnson understood so well and that are having a dangerously corrosive impact on the health and principles of American society. When the 1980s began, about 26 million Americans—around 10 percent of our entire population—lived below the poverty level as officially defined by the government: an annual income of about $12,000 or less for a family of four. (The average is now under $10,000.) By the end of our decade of "prosperity," the number of impoverished had swollen to more than 30 million, comprising an even higher proportion of the American people. And the numbers have continued to increase. Poverty afflicts people of every race, although there are more poor whites than poor blacks. Most of the poor, after all, are much like you and me. They want to work, to earn a decent living, and give their kids a chance. Many dream of finding a way to escape. But few succeed; and those who do come from among the brightest, most determined, and most fortunate of their fellows. But a society that offers opportunity to only a handful of the most exceptional is not a just society. (Were the same standard applied to the middle class, the streets of every town and suburb would be overflowing with the idle.)

Although poverty can be found almost everywhere—from the potato-growing counties of northern Maine to the cottonfields of rural Mississippi—large numbers of the impoverished are our neighbors, confined to small sections of our inner cities ominously called ghettos. And most of them are black. Few have any chance of escape from decaying neighborhoods. And during the years that have intervened since

Johnson's hopeful proclamation an entire generation has come of age whose conduct and values have been shaped by the culture of the city streets—including, for many, the use of drugs, which are, as Jacques Attali observes, "the nomadic substance of the millennial losers, of the excluded and the discarded. They provide a means of internal migration, a kind of perverse escape from a world that offers none."

Incorporating the black poor into American society will require measures different in nature and dimension from those we have discussed. Abandoned by their fellow citizens, despairing of escape, many have rejected the institutions and principles of the nation they inhabit. They do not vote. They do not participate in the common life. Some work, but many who would like jobs cannot find them in a declining economy. And a life that is little more than a struggle for survival provides little opportunity or incentive to acquire abilities that even a growing economy might reward.

In 1966, President Johnson pledged that "we will not permit any part of this country to be a prison where hopes are crushed, human beings chained to misery, and the promise of America denied." Proposals to implement this pledge were formulated and the first tentative steps toward implementation were begun. Then the shattering war in Vietnam absorbed the energies of leadership, the resources of the country, and, finally, the moral purpose of the American people. The result was a disaster, not only for black Americans, but for the entire society and its founding principles of justice and freedom. The population of our urban prisons grew, even as the walls were heightened and fortified by growing injustice, bigotry, and fear. We created a nation within the nation, its people shut off from the opportunities open to white America. And, in many cities, as the black population increased, whites fled to surrounding towns, abandoning their fellow citizens to lives of almost unimaginable poverty and a desperate struggle for survival which had never been part of the American promise.

Shortly after the triumphant passage of the Voting Rights Act of 1965, President Johnson told his staff that "voting rights are important, but it's only the tail on the pig, when we ought to be going for the whole hog. . . . The problem's not just civil rights. Hell, what good are rights if you don't have a decent home or someone to take care of you when you're sick? Now, we've got to find a way to let Negroes get what most white folk already have. At least the chance to get it. As I see it, the problem isn't so much hatred as fear. The white worker fears the Negro's going to take something away from him—his job, his house, his daughter. Well, we ought to do something about that. Now we can't do everything at once, but we can make people feel a little guilty about not doing anything about it. We've got the biggest pulpit in the world up here, and we ought to use it to do a little preaching."

The preaching soon stopped—or, rather, it was turned toward more remote and implausible goals. Nor was fear the only obstacle. Blacks must confront barriers that other minorities have not faced. The ambition for education and success that has allowed me some measure of personal achievement was derived from ancestors who transmitted a cultural tradition established for over two millennia. The same is true for almost all those who have migrated to this country. Blacks alone were brought here by force, severed from their native culture, denied the rudiments of education and the ability to sustain a family life by the methodical brutalities of slavery. For a century after Emancipation they were forcibly kept apart from American society by a formally legalized apartheid. The civil-rights movement of the 1960s abolished the legal forms of racial bigotry, but could not restore a cultural tradition that had been shattered by centuries of hatred and despair.

Men and women of all races are born with the same range of abilities. But, far too often, the native capacities of black Americans are impaired by ruptured family life, decaying and violent neighborhoods, a school system incapable of cultivating the talent or imparting the knowledge necessary for achievement in modern America. From their infancy through their maturity the realities of ghetto life and the indifference of white society conspire to prevent African Americans from escaping a prison whose walls are invisible to the sight but solid and unbreachable to the mind. Nor do children of other races experience the lacerating pain of white hatred or prejudice or condescension. Other minorities have subdued similar hostilities by their success in a variety of occupations. But achievement does not change the color of a person's skin. Nor have others been excluded because they were black—a form of hostility whose intensity is matched by no other prejudice in our society.

Unless we are willing to confront the consequences of our racism and act to overcome them, the downward spiral will continue: unemployment and poverty breeding despair; despair creating indifference to the education that offers the only hope of escape; and the fusion of despair and indifference leading toward a destructive rebellion against the fabric of society.

How have we allowed this to happen, and why? This predicament violates the most fundamental principles of our freedom and the teachings of every faith. And it is self-destructive. For if we continue to incarcerate black Americans in strongholds of poverty and hopelessness, the entire nation will be diminished. If millions are deprived of opportunity, then the opportunity for all Americans will be reduced. Indeed, it has already begun to happen.

No series of programs can restore hope, ambition, or a realistic expectation of personal achievement to the large majority of those citizens—especially the young—who are compelled to inhabit the country within a country we call the ghetto. For most, no transformation of the educational system, no best-intentioned efforts by men and women of goodwill can overcome the realities of ghetto life. The ubiquity of drugs, the omnipresent menace of violence, the broken homes, the absence of structures to instill values compose the realities of neighborhood life. These inescapable conditions of daily existence shape the attitudes and actions of inner-city residents far more than any government programs do. Their values, status, and expectations are irrevocably contoured by the world in which they live, a world whose very existence is a tangible and vehement reproof to all Americans.

Since no externally imposed program can work a redeeming transformation within the ghettos, the only solution left is to dismantle them. We should take two very different but equally essential approaches to this task of reconstruction. The first would be a return to the philosophy of the Demonstration Cities Program of 1966, suggested by Walter Reuther and initiated (but not completed) by President Johnson. This program would not be restricted to models but would be directed toward rebuilding our most devastated urban areas. Its underlying principle, confirmed by experience, is the futility of a piecemeal, fragmented assault on urban programs. Housing, education, job creation, law enforcement are all part of a larger whole: the creation of a city that provides the essential amenities of a civilized existence and economic opportunity for its inhabitants.

Community leaders, both public and private, would formulate integrated plans for urban reconstruction and be required to mobilize whatever resources are available for its implementation. Such a plan, once approved at the federal level, would receive assistance from the national government, and a federal coordinator would be appointed to make sure the plan was being followed and to minimize the inevitable waste, graft, and corruption. There is, after all, no housing problem or education problem or job problem. There is only the problem of the cities, and since this problem is different in Atlanta than in New York or Chicago or Boston, different plans are required. All, however, would have one thing in common: the necessity of strong and committed community leadership. In many, perhaps most cases, this will require the participation of the towns that now encircle the central city. Plans must encompass the entire metropolitan area that depends on the city for much of its commercial activity, and that often supplies essential resources, such as water and power, to the urban center. One can have a city without suburbs, but without the city even the most affluent suburbs would soon begin to wither. Although the citizens of some metropolitan areas may be reluctant to become involved in the solution of urban problems (after all, urban problems are why they left in the first place), their participation can be mandated by state law and by imposing appropriate conditions on federal assistance. Clearly it is both unjust and self-defeating to impose the task of providing equal opportunity on lower-income whites who have remained in the cities, a course that has proven a certain route to increased racial enmity and to violence. In the end, of course, even the more distant and affluent inhabitants of the metropolitan area will reap the benefits of improvement in the quality of urban life, just as a continued deterioration must, in time, reach even to their gated lawns.

Urban reconstruction on the scale needed will take time. But we cannot afford to sacrifice still another generation to the debilitating ravages of poverty. Therefore, our approach will also be designed to encourage a kind of migration, a voluntary abandonment of the inner cities in search of that same opportunity that, beginning in the 1940s, stimulated the Great internal movement of blacks from the rural South to Northern urban centers.

We should establish, in various parts of the country, residential work and learning programs for inner-city youths. Such programs are analogous to the Civilian Conservation Corps, the National Youth Administration, and the Works Progress Administration, which helped to train and employ victims of the Great Depression. Those who choose to enter such programs would have to make a commitment to continuous residence over a substantial period of time. They would perform productive labor, at minimum compensation, while at the same time receiving guidance and training from men and women equipped to teach a variety of skills and basic academic subjects.

By leaving the destructive environment of the inner cities, young people would at least have a chance to develop skills and learn the satisfactions of useful work, perhaps even to begin to challenge the values that threaten to destroy their lives. Some would be prepared for more advanced vocational training. Others would be taught the skills and knowledge necessary to prepare them for further education. With luck, and if the programs are realistically designed to enhance opportunity, a large number would never return to the urban caldrons that are already consuming their lives. The same or similar programs would be made available to the many poor who live outside the inner cities, except that if they are within commuting distance of work and learning programs, and demonstrate a high level of commitment, it may not be necessary for them to depart their environments.

"Give no bounties," wrote Ralph Waldo Emerson, "make equal laws: secure life and property and you need not give alms. Open the doors of opportunity to talent and virtue, and they will do themselves justice, and property will not be in bad hands." Of course, Emerson was an optimist. But his observation contains an important truth, whose disregard has damaged the poor, increased enmity between income groups, and weakened the economy by intensifying the exclusion of the impoverished.

Welfare must be one of the most degrading programs ever devised for the humiliation and oppression of our fellow human beings. "When you're on welfare," Senator Daniel Patrick Moynihan once wrote, "it's almost a complete collapse. . . . You're a pauper. Your whole life is broken up. You're dealing with brain-dead, artery-clogged bureaucracies that hate you." And it is worse than that. Welfare is not only a degradation, it is a payoff, a small handout in return for silence, for abstinence from vocal or violent protest. Therefore:

We should abolish the iniquitous welfare system, but only after work and training programs are in place. For welfare is a public dole, which simply transforms citizens into dependents, strips them of their dignity, robs them of respect from their children, and destroys the incentive to prepare for useful labor. Some, of course, are unable to learn or work: the elderly, the handicapped, the very young. These will continue to need support to sustain life. For the rest, jobs and learning—not welfare and relief—if not the answers for all, are the only hope for reopening the doors of opportunity to the justly despairing poor. And if the doors are open, many will enter.

Residential work and training centers will cost money, of course. Yet similar programs were funded a half-century ago from a far more seriously depressed economy. And they worked. But such programs and centers are not a giveaway or a free ride. They are an investment in the skills that are the foundation of an advanced economy, and in the creation of new consumers whose income will help support profitable production. If we are not willing to invest in our people, then our greatest natural resource will continue to decay, leading us toward even more serious distress.

Once we provide training and work programs, we cannot realistically expect that all the poor will successfully acquire working skills or decent jobs. But suppose half do. Suppose 15 million more people are enabled to contribute to our economic growth. If they spent like most working Americans, they would add at least $75 billion in consumption to the economy each year. They also would contribute to production. My proposal is a bargain. Even better, enactment would signify a return to reason by a society that seems to prefer a poor population that drains the economy to one whose progress would enlarge it.

For such programs to succeed, private enterprise must take a leading role—with government cooperation and funding readily available. Business is more likely to succeed than are public institutions. It has the resources, and the experience in training people for productive labor. It can, more readily than government, enforce the discipline necessary to ensure that only those committed to learning and training are allowed to remain. And for those who participate, business—not government—will seem more like the real world, providing a daily, tangible reminder of possibility, offering contact with the conditions and attitudes of those who work for a living.

Business also has something to gain. It will need workers, and those who already know the job and the company will be especially valuable. Even if some feel, and quickly conceal, a slight revulsion when the citizens of poverty first appear in their centers, this feeling will soon dissolve in the awareness that they are all connected, more firmly than they may have believed, by a common humanity and a shared allegiance to a great country. Everyone will feel better and everyone will do better—a combination that is the rarely experienced essence of American desire.

EDUCATING A MODERN WORK FORCE

It is no secret to most parents and concerned citizens that our public school system is a disaster. Not all schools, of course. Not all the time. But many, perhaps most, acting in dutiful obedience to law, incarcerate young children in classrooms until they depart several years later with only the most rudimentary verbal and scientific knowledge, and with few, if any, skills to exchange for work that promises an expanding future.

The responsibility for the decay of American education cannot be assigned to teachers. Nearly all of them are trying their best in a system that deprives them of essential resources, devalues their importance to the community, smothers initiative under large and inflexible school bureaucracies, assigns too many children to a classroom, and in some systems—often in our large cities—makes it clear that school boards and administrators are more concerned with a child's orderly progress through the grades than with what happens to the student's mind on the journey.

Education is today's gateway to American opportunity. There are no more New England forests to subdue, no

Western frontier left to conquer. Opportunity is now contained within a settled society. It is more easily attained by those who have mastered the knowledge and skills that sustain the modern economy. Moreover, if education can give opportunity, lack of education can take it away. The receding demand for unskilled and uneducated labor has already swelled the ranks of the impoverished, and widened the income division between classes. Yet the reality is that America's most valuable natural resource is a skilled and educated people. Our failure to cultivate this resource undermines our ability to compete in a world where productivity and innovation require an increasingly skilled work force. Our foreign competitors, understanding that the economic future depends upon ability and knowledge, have assigned a top priority to the quality of education. And it is paying off. Japanese workers, for example, demonstrate a level of technical sophistication far above that of a few decades ago. Both in the Far East and in Europe, young students have already surpassed their American counterparts in the mastery of several disciplines. A recent survey by a presidential commission concluded that on nineteen international assessments of student achievement, American students never ranked first or second. Compared only with students from other industrialized countries, American students ranked last seven times.

Our neglect of education has already contributed to decline. Many American companies, for example, have established manufacturing operations overseas because they find foreign workers more productive. The earliest advocates of free public education in America argued that teaching our youth would make them productive members of society. The students would eventually staff our industry and buy our products. The question was debated by state legislatures across the country. Everywhere proponents asserted that education would be the cornerstone of American prosperity and ensure the lasting strength of democratic government. And it worked. A well-educated work force has always returned the cost of learning manyfold through increased productivity and an expanding market. And democracy has withstood every assault.

However, simply providing more money to existing school systems will not, by itself, make them better. Admittedly, schools need decent physical facilities. Teachers should be well paid. But money alone does not improve the quality of education. Often it simply strengthens an entrenched educational bureaucracy that is resistant to change. Almost thirty years ago, this very issue was debated in the White House by those formulating the first bill to provide federal aid to education. Some, ultimately victorious, wished simply to help fund existing school systems. A second group argued that a substantial amount of money should be directed to educational research centers, which would devise model curricula and textbooks and then make its products available to schools across the country. The assumption of this second group was that most teachers wanted to teach well. They wanted their students to learn. But, as in any skilled occupation, only a few were gifted with extraordinary natural talents. The rest, if motivated—and most teachers are motivated—could improve their effectiveness with training and assistance. Decades of experience have resolved that debate. We spend a great deal on education, and yet the quality of learning continues to decline. Money alone offers no solution. Obviously a drastically new approach is necessary. Therefore:

We should establish a series of educational research centers to develop curricula for teaching basic skills and knowledge, and to write textbooks that, eliminating dependence on rote memory, stimulate students to experience the joy of discovery for themselves. This is not an impossible task. Groups at the Massachusetts Institute of Technology and other institutions have developed just such texts in mathematics and physics. We know how to teach. We just don't do it.

Since simply publishing research will accomplish little, we should augment these educational research centers with the creation of an educational extension service. This service would, on request, send out men and women to explain and demonstrate the results of expert research to individual teachers in their own classrooms. The use of new techniques and materials would be decided by the individual teacher or by local school authorities. This educational extension service would resemble the original program of agricultural extension, which, farmer by farmer, demonstrated the advantages of crop rotation, irrigation systems, and other scientific techniques of cultivation. Through this rather tedious process, American agriculture was revolutionized, becoming the most productive in the world.

We should also provide an alternative to present secondary-school education for those many students whose needs and special skills are outside the range of traditional education. An apprenticeship program—like those already successful in other countries—offers just such an alternative. Young men and women should be able to apprentice themselves to skilled machinists, toolmakers, electricians, construction workers. They would be compensated for their work, but at a relatively low level. At the end of their apprenticeship they would be awarded a certificate or diploma equivalent in status to a high school degree, formally qualifying them to work at the skill or trade they had chosen or to pursue further education. For the students, such a program would increase confidence in their future opportunity for rewarding employment. And America's pool of skilled labor would have been increased. (A similar program is now conducted in Germany, with results that have enhanced the German economy.) Apprentices enrolled in this program would also be required to take some academic courses, schooling them in the basics of American history, government, and literature. Thus, they would have an opportunity to transfer to regular secondary schools if their intellectual interests developed in that direction. This program would be largely conducted by private business, with government supervision to ensure that skills were being taught and that apprentices were fulfilling the work and academic standards of the program. For business the advantages are large: a corps of inexpensive labor during the period of apprenticeship, and access to a pool of trained and skilled workers at the end of the line.

In examining this or any other agenda for change, we cannot and should not evade the fact that an endeavor to renew democratic capitalism will be expensive. And the American people will have to pay that cost. The luxury of denying this reality is reserved for politicians whose public discourse does not require any firm connection to the truth. Having accepted the painful necessity that constructive change will require some financial sacrifice by the majority of Americans, we should be equally aware that failure to act will ultimately be far more costly in terms of declining income and a deteriorating standard of life.

Some of the proposals in this essay, which call for changes in the legal structure governing both the economic and political process, will not require any expenditure except one of will and energy in active pursuit of common goals. In some instances imagination and creativity will prove more effective than money. However, many programs will be expensive, including some of those designed to help businesses modernize and expand, and those intended to extend opportunity to those now denied it and to expand it for those whose opportunities have been diminished. It will be costly to restore the infrastructure and redefine it to include organized technological innovation, and to provide individual citizens with the skills and knowledge needed to work effectively in a modern economy.

Some of this cost will be paid in the form of higher prices for goods produced by businesses that must bear some or all of the expense of modernization and expansion and therefore will be compelled to add some of this increase to prices in order to maintain earnings sufficient to continue and to strengthen the enterprise.

Some will come from those who are stripped of government subsidies and contracts that are thought unjust or that interfere with competition in an open market. Some of the money will be supplied from that mysterious reservoir of resources on which the government seems able to draw whenever the need seems urgent enough, like the hundreds of billions allocated for the salvation of failed financial institutions. And some will require increases in taxation. This necessity will undoubtedly provoke the greatest resistance. And such resistance is understandable. Today's opposition to new or higher taxes reflects widespread apprehension about the future, increasing personal insecurity, and distrust of a government that has wasted and abused the public wealth. To many, paying taxes is equivalent to depositing money with a known embezzler.

Yet our failing economic system has already imposed huge new taxes on the great majority of Americans. They do not appear in the tax code or on annual returns. Instead, they have been levied in the form of lost income and diminished possibilities for future increase. Had the income growth that occurred during the quarter-century after the Second World

War been continued, the average family income would be twice what it is today. That means our economic decline has already imposed a 50 percent tax on the average working American. Stagnation and decline have already taken a heavy toll on the standard of American life, and should it continue, it will be far more costly than any conceivable rise in taxation.

Proposed changes in the structure of democratic capitalism are designed to enhance our ability to increase wealth and to give every citizen the opportunity to share in the fruits of renewed national growth. Taxes dedicated to such a purpose, if successful, will enrich the lives of every citizen and create even larger possibilities for later generations. They are not merely an expense. They are an investment in the well-being of our citizens and the greatness of our democracy. Admittedly such future benefits must be paid for in the present. But we have let too much go too wrong for too long. And remedy is always more costly than prevention. We must either sacrifice now—and it will not be painless—or allow a further deterioration in the quality of American life whose cost to the country and its people defies calculation.

The real question is not taxation, but our willingness to accept the burden of a struggle to continue America's progress. Were we attacked by a foreign enemy, who can doubt our response? This may not be a war. But it is a battle to preserve American principles and the individual opportunity that is the American promise. Defeat will inflict serious damage on the Republic. And even though success is not certain, there is no alternative to making the effort.

I have little doubt that if this is made clear, the American people will be ready to respond. William James once said this country needed a "moral equivalent of war," by which, I suppose, he meant a common purpose that could unite us in a common endeavor. We found this when confronted by the crisis of the Great Depression. Though now dormant, that sense of purpose can be reawakened in the struggle to heal and restore America. If our people, whose suspicion of public action has grown, can be brought to trust such a cause—both the sincerity of its intentions and the moral integrity of its leaders—they will overthrow the structure of decline and oppression, and construct a new America founded on those ancient and tested principles that have made us a great nation.

Structural changes that increase our ability to create wealth ensure a just distribution of income, extend opportunity to the poor and learning to the young, and will strengthen the entire American economy. They are the answer—at least part of the answer—to the prospect of continuing deterioration. All of us want to preserve and enhance the greatness and freedom of the nation. But though America is real, it is also an abstraction. At any one time, the country is made up of and reflects the values of those who inhabit it. And today's citizens seek the same opportunity as those who first set foot on the wild shores of a new world: to be free, to work, to improve the conditions of life.

Today that opportunity is being diminished for many and denied to some, a fact that is both cause and consequence of our present distress, and that provides both the necessity and goal of change. For it is the promise of America which is at stake.

"I don't believe in a law to prevent a man from getting rich," President Lincoln told an audience in New Haven, "it would do more harm than good. So while we do not propose any war upon capital, we do wish to allow the humblest man an equal chance to get rich with everybody else. When one starts poor, as most do in the race of life, free society is such that he knows he can better his condition; he knows that there is no fixed condition of labor, for his whole life. . . I want every man to have the chance."

This principle, set forth by the greatest of our moral leaders, is the inviolable standard for judgment on our own actions. Although the intervening century has brought an immensity of growth and complexity to economic activity that neither Lincoln nor his audience could have imagined, the precept is as fixed in the meaning of America as the continent itself: that all, equally, shall have the opportunity to advance themselves, and that none are condemned, without hope of escape, to lives of misery and needless suffering. Providing that chance is the principal objective of our movement for democratic capitalism.

V

Promises to Keep

WHEN THE SIGNERS of the Declaration of Independence asserted that "all men" were "endowed . . . with certain unalienable rights," they did not mean that such rights were natural constituents of humanity, like the need for food, or an instinct for survival. They were expressing a moral purpose and a political intent. The members of the Continental Congress who convened in Philadelphia to adopt this declaration knew that most of the world's people were confined under various forms of autocratic or despotic rule, that all but a handful were irrevocably consigned to a life that was "nasty, brutish, and short." The nation they hoped to form would be different, a democratic republic, designed to give the people themselves the power to secure and preserve their right to "Life, Liberty, and the Pursuit of Happiness."

That brief phrase was a compendium, almost a metaphor, for far more extensive convictions. In a few felicitous phrases, which history would apotheosize, it compressed the whole meaning and promise of America, addressed not only to our own people but to all countries. "Liberty" was the individual's right to share in government, to receive justice, and to be protected from arbitrary power even if exercised in obedience to the will of a majority. "The Pursuit of

Happiness" included what we later came to call opportunity, the chance to seek personal fulfillment, to sustain binding ties with our fellow citizens. Eighty-five years after its proclamation, Lincoln, speaking at Independence Hall, reflected that the "sentiments embodied in the Declaration of Independence" were "that which gave promise that in due time the weights should be lifted from the shoulders of all men, and that *all* should have an equal chance."

Those "unalienable rights" were elaborated and secured by the Constitution and laws of the dawning Republic. Later, change and growth would require many alterations in the conduct of democracy: Slavery was abolished; economic monopolies were prohibited; women were enfranchised; all citizens obtained the right to vote; the organization of labor was secured by law. But none of these changes were inconsistent with our founding principles. Indeed, they sustained and enhanced them against assaults from the inevitable changes of sentiment and condition that arise from history's passage.

Although the mandates of the American catechism have occasionally been attacked or violated in domestic conflict and in foreign wars, after two centuries they still endure. They are still what we mean by "America." From our earliest years, these principles made us an exemplar of freedom to the oppressed of the world, and later encouraged millions to sever ancestral ties to seek a home among us; as our strength increased, they persuaded us that our now unmatched might had imposed a responsibility to protect the freedom of distant peoples. Today, partly because of our example, our power, and our efforts, the legendary words of our founders have helped to guide millions seeking to forge new democracies from old tyrannies.

The constitutional structure we built on these principles has brought a growing prosperity to the country, and a better life—improving from generation to generation—to nearly all our people. That achievement was also among our hopes and purposes from the beginning. Admittedly, we had inherited abundant resources and were to be gifted with men and women of great ingenuity. But the same is true of other lands now mired in poverty and disarray. Our growth was made possible by democratic rule sustained by principles of opportunity and justice. On that foundation we built a great nation.

Yet, as we have seen, that progress is now gravely endangered. The grand vessel, America, is under savage assault, not from foreign foes, but from within. The standard of life for most Americans is in decline. After two centuries, the promise of a society where all may share increasing opportunity is being dissolved. Nor is our present condition a short-term dip in some deceptive economic chart. We may, perhaps, experience occasional interludes of improvement. But such a "recovery" will only benefit a small proportion of Americans, and it will be brief. For there is no escape from a relapse into decline. Our present distress is not an aberration. It results from a long process of decay in the supporting structures of our political and economic system. That system, the democratic capitalism that has been the source of American growth and freedom, is being eroded by greed, corruption, and the failure of enterprise to adapt to the exigencies of a changing world economy. Thus, deterioration in the quality of American life will continue, unless and until we act to avert it.

In the decades between the mid-1940s and the 1960s, it became fashionable to speak of the "American century," an arrogant phrase that signified our claim to leadership of the future. Yet unless we join in demanding and forcing significant change, the period that spans the years between our victory in the Second World War and our doomed struggle in Vietnam may have marked, not the beginning, but the end of the American century—that enormous growth in wealth, individual well-being and opportunity, and power that began after the Civil War.

The flaws that are the source of our present distress are a result of our departure from those founding principles on which we defined and built a nation: Opportunity has been closed or significantly diminished for millions. Justice has been denied by a system that has allowed the depredations of the rich and powerful to draw wealth from the hands of an increasingly besieged middle class. Liberty itself has been impaired by our failure to formulate an effective response to the epidemic of violent crime which has bred fear and insecurity, and whose continued rise will evoke a demand for repression. These transgressions—only a few examples of abandoned principle—are not only the result of neglect, mistakes, and incompetence. They originate, as I have pointed out, in the failure of our economic structure to meet the challenges of a competitive market, combined with the increased domination of the political process by large concentrations of private wealth.

The founding principles of democratic capitalism—private enterprise within a competitive market—have been distorted to give advantage, not to those who can provide the most jobs or enhance the general welfare, but to those who can manipulate the governing structure of wealth and politics to aggrandize themselves at the expense of the people. And although the forms of democratic rule have been carefully maintained, the elected caretakers of the American community have allowed much of the authority to conduct the affairs of the country to fall into the hands of a small but powerful minority, many of whom are now relatively free to pursue their own interests without regard to the aspirations, beliefs, and interests of the American community. As a result, representative democracy itself has been impaired, endangering not only the economy, but the freedom of the people. The Founding Fathers foresaw this possibility as a major threat to democracy, and our experience has reaffirmed their wisdom.

Aware that even the most carefully constructed protections of government might be unable, or unwilling, to guard the general interest, the Framers bestowed ultimate sovereignty on the people. Thus, only the people have the power to mount an attack on the sources of distress and reshape the deeply flawed structure of democratic capitalism. It is possession of that supreme power that gives them the right and the duty to act.

Even though their sovereignty was institutionalized in "the restraint of frequent elections," the people's power does not reside just in the election-day ballot. It is far more substantially established by the pervasive awareness that no judgment is final and a time of decision is always close. "Before the sentiments, impressed on their mind by the mode of their elevation can be effaced by the exercise of power," Madison wrote, defending constitutional limits on tenure in office, "they will be compelled to anticipate the moment when their power is to cease, when their exercise of it is to be reviewed, and when they must descend to the level from which they were raised; there forever to remain unless a faithful discharge of their trust shall have established their title to a renewal of it."

It was this potent and inescapable outgrowth of the requirement of "frequent elections" which, a century later, led Lincoln to regard as self-evident that "in this country, public sentiment is everything. With it, nothing can fail; against it nothing can succeed." That "sentiment"—now called public opinion—is still decisive if it can be mobilized in support of a cause firmly rooted in awareness of the country's distress and responsive to the experiences, observations, and difficulties of the people's daily life.

The entire history of America is crowded with demonstrations of this truth. To arrest the growing danger of Federalist tyranny, Jefferson and his allies joined to form a new party, which, in 1800, took the White House from the party of George Washington. Later renamed the Democratic party, it has endured to the present day. The Progressive movement, the Populist movement, the antislavery movement, the Anti-Imperialist League, the modern civil-rights and women's movements are only a few instances of organized efforts to protect American principles against assault or to adapt democratic values to changing circumstances. Many of them succeeded—not completely, but enough to make important and liberating changes in American life.

If the people, faithful to this enduring political tradition, join to demand, openly, vocally, and through concerted action, that America be restored to its founding principles, restoration will come. That demand must be large, organized, and unified in pursuit of a common purpose: that America, and those who govern it, whether through public office or through the power of private wealth, serve the needs of all the citizens and the greatness of our democracy.

To that end, I propose a movement of democratic capitalism to restore and strengthen the structure that allowed the nation to flourish. It will not be easy to mobilize such a movement. The problems are large; their resolution will be difficult. But human skills can heal the destruction wreaked by human hands. The more programmatic proposals contained in the preceding sections of this essay are intended only as evidence of this possibility, not as a comprehensive agenda. They must certainly be amended, enlarged, and synthesized into themes that every citizen can comprehend.

For such a movement to have any hope of success, it must

enlist the energies of a people unified in a common purpose. Today that necessary unity is obstructed by the increasing fragmentation of American society. The historic American motto, *E pluribus unum* ("Out of many, one"), a statement of both principle and purpose, is being inverted by those widening fissures between races and ethnic minorities and, most damagingly, between income groups, which are transforming us into a class society against the expectations and most hopeful prophecies of our nation's founders.

Those who now govern understand that maintaining divisions between Americans has helped an elite reap wealth and power from our deepening distress. The 1988 presidential campaign was dominated by the televised picture of a black killer, skillfully contrived to intensify the fears of white America. It is a classic tactic of the political right to set poor whites against blacks, or low-income workers against the impoverished, thus freeing the powerful to divert our resources to themselves. Based on a lie, it is a sin.

There can be no popular will when the varied groups that compose America feel isolated from others who share many of their grievances and their fears. Yet an effective expression of democratic power requires its shared exercise. If there is no unity of purpose or belief, then power will move toward those anxious and willing to use it. And so it has. Thus, our present divisions have made it more difficult to mobilize a movement through which our people can exert their power toward common goals.

But the difficulty is not insuperable. Indeed, it may yield more readily than we suppose. For even though division is real, it has been created from falsehood. The distress of all aggrieved groups flows from similar causes. Their plight is not the fault of others in distress. My optimism rests not on wishful thinking, but on a conviction from experience that these truths, if forcefully explained, can overcome divisions that are based on lies and that damage only those who are severed from their fellow citizens. From the reality that separation is destructive and debilitating to the prospects of every group, it is possible to create a bond that will sustain a unity of effort.

Let us illuminate this premise by a brief glance at the emergent "classes" of a nation that once proudly claimed to be classless.

To borrow a recent metaphor from Robert Reich, during the Depression of the 1930s we were nearly all on a down escalator. Now some ride upward, glancing across the bordering rail curiously—not without a certain sympathy, an occasional twinge of compassion—at the passengers jammed aboard the descending mechanical stairs. Yet an increasing number of the more thoughtful and foresighted among the fortunate understand that their own ascent is in danger, that the economy that has treated them so well cannot long survive the immiseration of the multitudes who compose the market and provide the workers on whom the creation of wealth is based. Nor does their own wealth totally insulate them from the other conditions that are diminishing the quality of American life. Even a limousine can be halted by an overcrowded roadway; the largest bank account does not deter the mugger; and great riches do not purchase either clean air or a substitute for the need to breathe. Admittedly, many of the more fortunate still believe that wealth and their own merits have allowed them a permanent exemption from the distress of their fellow citizens. They are wrong, of course. In the long run, there cannot be many Americas moving in different directions. But their error has not prevented their domination of public power, with its substantial ability to protect their interests against threatening change. This influence has corrupted the democratic process. And it has made some people very rich. Few among them are likely to join our movement, although there will be some surprising exceptions.

Most of the more than 30 million impoverished Americans learn at a very early age that almost no one really cares enough to help them find a permanent exit. Their sense of estrangement is not illusory. They are truly abandoned by American society, outcasts in their own land, and thus they seek other ways to establish the reality of their existence. More than twenty years ago, a presidential commission predicted that if we failed to act decisively, and soon, we would evolve into two countries—one white and one black, separate and unequal. We did nothing. And it has all come true. Except even that body of caring men could not foresee that poor whites, Hispanics, and Asians would also be condemned to the other, lesser America, so that even the community of the poor would be shattered by mutual distrust and hatred.

The immensity of this estrangement, the widening gulf between cultures, income groups, and races, the sensed impotence and abandonment will make a unity of purpose difficult to achieve. Yet most of the poor of all races and cultures are victims of the same flaws in the structure that have adversely altered the shape of life for nearly all Americans. Concealed beneath advancing separation and distrust is a common interest. And a shared interest is the foundation of shared effort. Since that foundation exists, unity is not impossible.

The poor will not be quick to join a movement of restoration. Distrust that has festered for decades will not yield easily. Still, when I traveled with Jesse Jackson through the rural South during his first presidential campaign in 1984, I watched the shining, almost adoring eyes of poor country folk, some whites mingled among the many blacks, as Jackson led them in a refrain: "I am somebody! I am somebody!"

Then, discarding the style of the preacher that he is, Jackson would lean over the lectern, extend his huge hands toward the audience, and, speaking in a subdued tone, confide that "these hands which picked cotton are going to pick a President." He didn't mean his own hands, of course, although all eyes had converged on them. He meant their hands. And they believed him. At least they wanted to believe him. It was almost miraculous: in the faces of the hopeless, hope had appeared. "Those folk don't want to be poor," Jackson told me afterward as we drove to his next stop. "And they'll work hard. Most of them. All they need is a chance they can believe in." But I had seen that myself, not only in the countryside but in poor city neighborhoods. The hope the poor seem to have lost is still there, buried, dormant, but not dead. It can be resurrected for a cause that will not just address their afflictions, but will fight to heal them. It won't be easy to persuade them. There have been many promises. Words won't do it. But actions will.

Above the poverty line but excluded from the ranks of the affluent (the 20 percent whose wealth has risen) is the working middle class, a group so large and diverse that it defies easy classification. This group has borne the principal burden of economic decline, suffered most from the manifold assaults on the American way of life. Yet, partly as consolation, partly because they are constantly reminded of the sins and idleness of the poor, partly because they resent the "handouts" given the destitute, partly because of racial bigotry, many refuse to admit that there is any common ground between them and those in poverty—that both are victims of the same forces and deficiencies that have so grievously harmed the nation.

Yet, one must not underestimate the good sense of the American worker. In 1968 Robert Kennedy spoke to a rally at a steel plant in Gary, Indiana. The hall was crowded with workers, mostly of Slavic descent, nearly all of whom were fiercely hostile toward black Americans. They knew Kennedy was an active supporter of civil rights and probably the white politician most admired by black Americans. Yet even though Kennedy did not dodge the issue of civil rights (nor did he stress it), they crowded to shake his hand, they cheered him clamorously, and, on primary day, they voted for him. They knew he was on their side. And that was all that mattered. That is all that ever matters to those who answer the whistle or go to the office: a fair day's pay for a fair day's work, and a leader who will take up their cause when injustice threatens.

A vigorous effort, honestly conceived and truthfully intended to advance the interests of divergent, even hostile groups, can bridge any division. You can't turn enmity into friendship. And "love thy neighbor" is a project for theologians. But people of different income classes and races will fight and work for a cause they believe is in their own interest, even if they have different reasons.

Jacques Attali, a distinguished French scholar and international banker long known as a friend to America, has recently written that our failures to confront and resolve our economic decay "are rooted in a profound cultural mutation" that "reflects a country abandoning those values for which it is so universally admired." He expresses from a distant vantage the same concerns that have led many Americans to conclude that many traditional values have been dangerously weakened, and some have been abandoned by large numbers of our fellow citizens. They will not be miraculously strengthened by the strident, and frequently self-seeking, invocations of politicians or evangelists. Even those who are truly moral leaders cannot, from pulpit or meeting hall, summon the country to renew and live by values deeply embedded in our history, in the precepts of our democracy, and in whatever spiritual faith we have. Values are not what we profess, but what we do. They exist only to the extent they define and prescribe the way in which we live, or strive to. Thus, for most of us—who are neither saints nor reprobates—our values are influenced by the circumstances of our existence and the conditions of society. In Eastern Europe, for example, we have seen how economic decay and political repression enhanced the values of liberty and economic justice so powerfully that long-established governments were toppled and states transformed. The same is true in America. Economic decline and social degeneration have impaired long-established values. The individual whose own way of life is endangered is likely to neglect his obligation to future generations. The business leader whose position and compensation depend on short-term changes in profits and stock prices is less inclined to invest in modernization and innovation whose benefits will not accrue for several years. A nation sundered into categories of income and race will not reestablish those bonds of neighborhood and community that have linked our lives to the lives of our fellows.

Our values are not lost. They have been submerged, in part, by the unexpected tides of decline and apprehension, by the steady erosion of opportunity and justice, and by the corruption of representative democracy. If these disorders can be arrested and reversed, then, given the opportunity and fulfill the promise of American freedom, values will reassert themselves, for they derive from the most fundamental needs of human fulfillment.

Although the more affluent members of the middle class have a better standard of living, they are divided—or feel divided—from other segments of American society, and from each other. Many are hostile toward or fearful of the black and the poor, contemptuous of the crudities of working-class life, separated in opinion and the experiences of daily life from many other middle-class citizens. Many resent giving the government tax money, which, if not wasted entirely, goes to support, they believe, a vast army of indolent citizens. Like many of us, stripped of binding social ties—neighborhood, community, an intimate group of friends—they strengthen their sense of self-worth by disdaining participation in projects and causes. Many of them are very lonely.

Yet their separation is not irrevocable. They too can be brought toward a common purpose. They want to believe. Despite their frequent expressions of helplessness or disdain, they still retain, even if they outwardly deny it, a desire to help restore the greatness of America. If they seem to turn away from the country's problems, it is because they have found no movement or organized cause in which they believe.

Should faith and patriotism not suffice, there is another and perhaps stronger bond. Over the past few decades the middle classes have found it harder and harder to sustain their standard of living. Although they have worked hard, often with some success, they have painfully witnessed the erosion of their hopes for a more abundant life; the dreams of youth blend into the grimmer realities of middle age. They also are directly affected by many of the deteriorations in American society: terrible schools, poisoned air, fear of violence. Although little more than half vote in federal elections, they go dutifully to the polls, not resigned, but frustrated and angered by their conviction that, whatever the outcome, those who govern them will have little concern for their problems and will not act to reverse either the country's decline or the fading fortunes of its citizens. Like other groups, they understand what the statistics prove—that something has gone awry with their own, personal piece of the American dream. The shining prospect that hard work and allegiance to treasured values will be rewarded has been displaced by the harsh realities of arrested growth and mounting injustice in the distribution of the nation's wealth. And a shared grievance is the most potent healer of division.

Although the fragmentation of society is an obstacle to the formation of a movement for the restoration of America, it is far from insuperable. There is a strongly founded basis for unity—common interests, common grievances, and common adversaries. The grievances of nearly all our citizens have a common source. Nearly all are victims of the declining standard of American life. And the stakes for all of us are high: nothing less than our right to "the Pursuit of Happiness." A cause and the leadership to sustain it, if such a cause is justly and persuasively conceived, will rally people who, at least for this purpose, will no longer identify themselves by race or income, but only as Americans. Perhaps then we can progress even further toward Lincoln's injunction that we "at all times remember that all American citizens are brothers of a common country and should dwell together in the bonds of fraternal feeling."

Since a movement for change requires unity of action, the divisions that have ruptured a people into many peoples have strengthened the most formidable obstacle to the mobilization of a popular movement: the widespread feeling that nothing can be done, that citizens are powerless to change the conditions of public life. Separation and isolation help to reinforce this belief. Yet power can be used only by those who wield it confidently. Thus impotence, even if illusory, breeds impotence. And a sense of impotence severs the nerve of action.

Over the years many have come to believe that those who hold the power of wealth and public office—that mysteriously fascinating, glittering band seen in the pages of popular magazines or on television—have little concern for their difficulties; that the powerful will not, perhaps cannot, restore to them the fullness of the American promise. Our failures of leadership in recent years, the rising domination of privilege and wealth, provide some justification for this belief—but not for the conclusion that we are impotent. The inadequacies and abuses of the powerful do not prove that we are powerless, only that we have not used our power to strip them of authority.

For, however widely felt it may be, impotence is an illusion. This is our country, and our entire history is proof that we have the power to change it. During this century we have overcome difficulties larger and more dangerous than those that now confront us. In 1940, a year before the attack on Pearl Harbor brought us into a war whose scale was unprecedented in human history, the United States was still in the Great Depression. Business and finance were virtually paralyzed, and unemployment was high. Even after the German attack on Poland in September 1939 had precipitated a general war in Western Europe, the United States was still nineteenth on the scale of world military powers, moving up to eighteenth only after Holland fell. Since rifles were unavailable, our soldiers trained with mops resting on their shoulders; jeeps and cars bore the label "tank" for purposes of armored maneuvers; and we had virtually no combat planes that were not obsolete.

After Pearl Harbor, with rapid mobilization imperative, President Roosevelt kept production facilities under private management. Government orders were negotiated through contracts that allowed business to make substantial profits, while proposals to draft men for defense work were rejected. A partnership was forged in which government ordered goods and supplied the capital, while private enterprise and labor conducted the process of production. The result, as is well known, was a miracle of production. By 1943, we had exceeded the total production of all Axis and Allied countries combined. During the war, the index of manufacturing more than doubled, as did corporate profits. In almost every industry—from airplanes and tanks to aluminum and synthetic rubber—targets thought absurdly high when established were met and exceeded. New methods to accelerate production were introduced. For example, in 1941 it took 244 days to build a *Liberty-*class cargo ship. Two years later the same ship was constructed in just forty-one days. Production advances were accompanied by a stream of technological and scientific innovation: ground-to-ground radar, jet aircraft, sulfa drugs, and, of course, nuclear power.

At war's end, we were the world's most productive nation and had accomplished an unprecedented redistribution of income that transformed America into a middle-class nation. And the number of blacks and women in the work force had been greatly increased. (Even though some of these gains were erased when the war ended, the seeds of our postwar civil-rights and women's movements had been planted.) Perhaps most important, the stimulus of wartime mobilization had given business a new flexibility and swept away bureaucratic restraints, enabling it to convert to civilian production swiftly and on a large scale. Within months, tank factories were turning out cars; artillery manufacturers were assembling refrigerators. Rebuilt and restructured by war, our economy would lead the country into a period of unprecedented growth and prosperity, which left us, a full quarter-century after our victory, the wealthiest and most powerful nation in the history of the world. And the total cost of the Second World War was only slightly more than the interest we now pay annually on our national debt.

Of course, the conduct of business under the conditions

of war required restrictions and provided opportunities not relevant to a civilian economy. Still, that wartime experience has important lessons for today. It demonstrated that under the pressure of necessity, and with the stimulus of participation in a common national effort, business could expand, adapt, innovate, and increase efficiency, thus surpassing its competitors, who were then its enemies. Private enterprise, in cooperation with government, proved it could do what it is now failing to do.

The struggle to renew America is not a war. Yet the stakes are just as high: the future of American freedom. The effort to secure that freedom will be costly, and sacrifice will be necessary. Attainment of success will require many to submerge their individual ambitions in an urgent national enterprise of large dimension and uncertain outcome. Perhaps such an enterprise is just what we need. Perhaps the restoration of America can provide that "moral equivalent of war" which many have sought as a way to reunite the community of America, and will allow a generation of Americans to feel pride, even nobility, by sharing in an endeavor to strengthen the homeland of freedom and to enlarge our own legacy for generations yet unborn.

We are equal in ability to our predecessors, bred to the same traditions, inheritors of the American will to achieve. We have resources enough, human and material, to renew America's passage toward greatness. The power of our sovereign people to change America still exists, formally incorporated into the Constitution and ratified by two centuries of history. Like some fabled genie, it need only be invoked and it will appear.

Every four years we look for a new savior, hoping that the election of one man or another, one party or the other, will point the way to salvation. It will not happen. Indeed, it cannot happen. The leaders we need will rise to power only after the people act—voice their demands for change and support those demands with a mass movement for the restoration of America and renewed fidelity to its founding principles.

The memorable leaders of our past—from Presidents in the White House to private citizens and students exhorting us from street corners and campuses—were not emissaries of some higher power, but vehicles and exemplars of the brighter side of the American character, whose qualities are manifested in the struggle for justice, for opportunity, for the fairness implicit in human equality, for democratic rule, for public restraints against the abuses of concentrated wealth and established power. Some of these people became famous. Others were lost to public recollection. But they were all leaders, and they rose to great heights not only because of their personal attributes, but because the nation itself was overflowing with a sense of great possibility, proud, even arrogant, about America's indisputable greatness, its preeminence among nations.

Nations, like individuals, are at their best when they believe in the possibility of achievement, however arduous or difficult the task. In our past, it has been this kind of America that sought out leaders of ability and profound conviction, individuals who would summon us to share in America's struggle toward a large, if undefinable, destiny.

During the half-century that separates the onset of the Great Depression from the end of the war in Vietnam, public leadership turned to knowledgeable men and women from outside government to help devise constructive answers to our problems. But today the ties between the world of ideas and the world of action have been severed. The result is a government guided by the latest journalistic clichés, or by polls purporting to measure popular judgment on issues that few fully comprehend. Democracy requires not obeisance to dubious statistical measures of opinion, but leadership willing to act in the interests of the nation as it conceives those interests. The final judgment of the people is reserved for the polling place.

Thus, government has become a barren arena where debate over great principles and the quest for serious solutions have been replaced by unremitting jockeying for political advantage. The American people increasingly, and sensibly, ignore the flood of banalities that resound through the once noble chambers of national discourse. Where Clay and Calhoun once debated the future of the Union, where Vandenberg and Taft clashed over our obligation to rebuild war-devastated Europe, today's leaders vie with one another to disclaim the desirability of racial "quotas," knowing full well there will be no quotas established; they earnestly analyze a complex Banking Reform Act (beware of all laws labeled "reform") that will, if passed, serve only to liberate financial institutions to commit further mistakes and misdeeds; they enact a program for the cities totally inadequate in both substance and scale to resolve America's urban problems.

And in the White House—the home of Jefferson and Lincoln, of Roosevelt and Truman, Eisenhower and Kennedy—there is no voice summoning the people to the sacrifice needed to rebuild America or proclaiming policies equal to the magnitude of our problems. Instead, writers are hired to improve the "image" of a warrior President as if words, new formulations for inaction, could substitute for policies and deeds.

Thus mediocrity is in the saddle and rides the nation.

Madison said it was the duty of a republic to guard one part of society against the injustices of the other part. But the present political structure, the engine of democratic rule, lacks the will, perhaps even the capacity, to embark on the large-scale effort necessary to heal the most serious, ultimately fatal, ills of our free society. Therefore, the only recourse, the only remaining instrument for fulfilling the "duty of a republic," is the ultimate power of the people to force change upon a resistant system.

We are, today, a more apprehensive and inward-turning people. And that, too, is reflected in the quality of our leaders. Yet we have the resources, human and material, to sustain America's voyage toward greatness. We just don't believe we can do it. If we can pierce the veil of doubt that obscures our true power, then we can mobilize and act to discard the mediocre, the corrupt, the self-seeking, and let the whole country hear the demand that America be recaptured for its people. If we do that, leaders with the ability to guide us toward victory will come forth.

It is no accident of history, or tribute to great rhetoric, that the line in Kennedy's inaugural address that concluded "ask what you can do for your country" was quickly embedded in the memory of an entire generation. It was what we wanted to hear. We regarded it not as a summons to arduous sacrifice, but as a promise that we might have an opportunity to participate in something far larger than our personal concerns, to share in the life of our country.

Perhaps Kennedy understood this from the beginning of his campaign. But I think full realization began to materialize on a chill fall night at the Ann Arbor campus of the University of Michigan. Our campaign plane arrived very late—long after midnight—to find that thousands of students had remained awake to hear and applaud the young senator, soon to be their President. Informed that the cafeteria had been kept open, Ted Sorensen and I, famished from a day that had begun over eighteen hours earlier, rushed to the dining table and did not watch Kennedy mount the steps of a college building to deliver a brief, impromptu address. Before we had reached dessert, another staff member rushed in to inform us, somewhat breathlessly, that "he's just proposed a 'Peace Corps.' " We were too tired to react. Fuller consideration of Kennedy's commitment would have to await a few hours' sleep.

Within days, more than seven hundred students at Michigan had signed up for the as yet nonexistent Peace Corps. And, in the weeks that followed, we would be flooded with mail from volunteers in every part of the country. Unexpectedly, Kennedy had aroused a hitherto concealed desire. It was one thing to tell young people they could make a difference. It was something else—much more—to offer them a tangible, specific instrument to fulfill those vague exhortations. "Every American has some of the dream in him," Johnson once said. The Peace Corps would allow many to transform that dream into the reality of action. And people loved it, as they would love it still—if we gave them the chance. People want to share in the public activities that have so large an effect on their private lives, knowing that participation also means influence. They want the power democracy bestows on its citizens. When it is denied them, they may withdraw, not out of an inner abdication, but because the doors have been locked, the blinds drawn, the driveway fenced. That reality is a reason to believe in the possibility of forming the movement America so desperately needs.

To join in such an endeavor is not only an opportunity. It is an obligation. In his Lyceum Address of January 27, 1838, almost a quarter-century before his elevation to the presidency, Lincoln explained the duty we inherited on the day we were born American: "In the great journal of things happening under the sun, we, the American people . . . find ourselves in the peaceful possession of the fairest portion of the earth as regards extent of territory, fertility of soil, and salubrity of climate. We find ourselves under the government of a system of political institutions conducing more essentially to the ends of civil and religious liberty than any of which the history of former times tells us. We, when mounting the stage of existence, found ourselves the legal inheritors of these fundamental blessings. We toiled not in the acquirement or establishment of them; they are a legacy bequeathed us by a once hardy, brave, and patriotic, but now lamented and departed race of ancestors. Theirs was the task (and nobly they performed it) to possess themselves, and through themselves, us, of this goodly land; and to uprear upon its hills and its valleys, a political edifice of liberty and equal rights; 'tis ours only to transmit these—the former, unprofaned by the foot of an invader; the latter, undecayed by the lapse of time and untorn by usurpation—to the latest generation that fate shall permit the world to know. This task of gratitude to our fathers, justice to ourselves, duty to posterity, and love for our species in general, all imperatively require us faithfully to perform."

The grandson of immigrants who had fled poverty, persecution, and hopelessness, I was given the opportunity to attend some of America's finest schools, and, in my twenties, to serve in the White House as assistant special counsel to the President of the United States. I was to remain in public life for several years before departing for somewhat more tranquil occupations.

I never forgot—no one could forget—how much the descendants of my immigrant ancestors, including myself and my children, owe this wonderful country to which we belong. In 1961, I joined the swelling crusade for a New Frontier. In 1964 and 1965, I helped to formulate the design for a Great Society. Those exhilarating years have passed into history. The country is different now, its difficulties changed in shape and dimension. The programs and policies then so hopefully designed will not resolve our present distress. As the times have changed, so have the necessities and direction of public action. I return to the 1960s of my youth only in memory. It was a time, like a few other moments in America, when many believed that history itself could be bent to the just needs of humanity. I believe that still. Thus, now, many years later, with words my only weapon, I have labored to write this modest and incomplete essay in hopes of arousing others to a quest for healing change. Not from a sense of obligation. But out of love— love for this great country, and a belief in its possibilities equal to that which has brought so many millions to the shores of hope.

ABOUT THE AUTHOR

RICHARD N. GOODWIN is a graduate of Tufts University and Harvard Law School. He has served as a law clerk to Supreme Court Justice Felix Frankfurter, and in 1960 was assistant to then Senator John F. Kennedy. In 1961, Goodwin became assistant special counsel to President Kennedy. He subsequently served as deputy assistant secretary of state for inter-American affairs. Later, he was named special assistant to President Lyndon B. Johnson. He created the Alliance for Progress for Kennedy, and the Great Society for Johnson. He is the author of several books, including *The American Condition* and *Remembering America*. He lives with his wife, Doris Kearns, in Concord, Massachusetts.